Recipes from an Italian Butcher

The Silver Spoon Kitchen

Recipes from an Italian Butcher

Roasting, Stewing, Braising

Introduction

Picture a plate of Milanese osso bucco on the table in front of you, the fragrance of the rich, braised, meltingly tender meat mingling with that of the subtle, earthy saffron risotto. Or *polpetti*, tiny meatballs in a richly fragrant tomato sauce, with freshly grated Parmesan melting into it. Italian dishes such as these deserve their place on the list of world-class meat recipes. But there is such rich diversity in the Italian approach to meat, so many more dishes from the peninsula and its islands that once you have tried a few, you will want to explore further.

Italy only became a unified country in 1871, and the *cucina*, although it shares much, reflects this in its distinctly regional character. Sheep are a huge part of the Italian larder, and although we might be familiar with the Sardinian sheep's cheese, pecorino, it's rare to find any lamb or mutton other than cutlets (chops) on a menu in an Italian restaurant. The huge variety of Italian pork products—sausages, hams, and *porchetta*—are familiar in our grocery stores and supermarkets, and we know about cooking pork in milk, perhaps, and plenty about ragùs (Bolognese sauce), but how many of us are aware of Italian Rabbit Stuffed with Olives (see page 150) or Wild Boar Skewers with Myrtle (see page 180)?

Italian ways with meat are wide and varied, and deserve to be better known, so this book explores three methods of cooking—roasting, stewing, and braising—that bring out the very best of all types of meat, and which are used to delicious effect in the Italian kitchen. *Recipes from an Italian Butcher* shows just how easy it can be to make simple and hearty meat dishes that are full of Italian flavor. Depending on the ingredients used and the cuts of meat chosen, these dishes can even be quick and inexpensive to make and no less delicious for it. Many can be prepared in advance and simply left to roast in the oven.

Roasting, stewing, and braising

Cooking meat is one of the oldest activities known to humankind. In prehistoric times, humans discovered that flame-cooked meat was easier to digest, tastier, and healthier. However, every cooking method has its own rules, and every cut of meat requires a different type of cooking.

Roasting: A technique involving oven-cooking in a Dutch oven (casserole) or on a skewer (for pork, lamb, poultry, and rabbit after marinating the meat in oil and aromatic herbs). Best cuts for roasting: Veal top round (rump), beef rib, leg of lamb, pork loin, or *capocollo*. The heat creates a golden brown crust, which retains the juices and keeps the meat tender.

Stewing: This involves slow cooking at simmering point in a deep Dutch oven with liquid covering half the meat. Browning the meat beforehand is not necessary. Cuts for stewing: Diced red or white meat (shoulder and neck cuts for beef and veal stews, goulash, fricassée, chicken, and rabbit stews). The result is meat that is very tender, somewhat like boiled meat, but tastier.

Braising: A technique that involves extended oven-cooking at moderate heat in a large pan with a lid or in a Dutch oven and a small amount of liquid (a marinade, the meat juices, or the cooking liquid), which is absorbed by the meat. Before cooking the meat in the oven, it should be browned in fat, along with the vegetables, and splashed with liquid, such as wine. Cuts for braising: Veal round (topside) or shoulder, red meats, and game.

The Italian meal

Italian meals are divided by course. There's the antipasto (which translates as "before the meal"), small nibbles to begin, the equivalent of pre-appetizers (pre-starters) at restaurants. The *primo* and *secondo* (first and second courses) are the foundation of both lunch and dinner—the *primo* is usually a small plate of pasta, rice, or equivalent, not the main event, but the essential appetizer. The *secondo* is the meat (or fish) main course. Vegetables play an essential part in the *secondo* too—the meats are usually combined with vegetables and flavored with herbs. Alongside the *secondo* comes the separately listed, but equally well considered *contorno*. The word, roughly, means "contours" in the sense of them shaping the meal. Even fried or broiled (grilled) meat or fish is usually served with a lovingly prepared *contorno*. This might be something as simple as Mashed Potatoes and Cabbage (see page 279), Glazed Carrots (see page 272), or Roasted Zucchini, Potatoes, and Tomatoes (see page 268). Alternatively, a salad might accompany a *secondo*, and these are as imaginative and delicious as cooked vegetable accompaniments. The Corn and Red Bell Pepper Salad on page 268, for example, is fresh, zingy, and earthy enough to complement and cut through any meat.

Cooking meat the Italian way

From the lush, alpine north to the sun-baked south, the ingredients and traditions of Italian cooking vary widely, offering a huge range of recipes and choices to the curious cook. What all of these traditions offer, though, is respect for the ingredients. Italian food is largely a peasant cuisine that makes the most of what's available, intensifying and stretching flavors into memorable meals with simple ingredients. So when the greatest of ingredients are available—a beautiful joint of venison, a fat goose—Italians do everything to make meals worthy of those high-quality raw ingredients.

For the sake of the environment, it would be better if we all made an effort to eat less meat, so making more of it when we do, just as the Italians have been doing for generations, makes sense. Eating large amounts of meat, especially red meat, is also unhealthy. However, eating high-quality meat in moderation and as part of a balanced diet, is quite the reverse. So, wherever possible, try to eat organic, free-range or free-roaming animals, a wider variety of breeds—perhaps try pheasant or guinea fowl, venison or wild boar—and simply choose your cut according to the recipe.

Some meats are leaner than others and all of the recipes that follow take this into account. In general, meats such as goose and duck are so fatty that you need to remove fat as they cook so that they will crisp up and not become greasy. Others, such as chicken and beef, need to be basted in their own juices to stay moist. Some, such as venison, are so lean that they will need fat added before or during cooking so they do not dry out.

Choosing meat

It's always better to buy free-range and organic meat if you possibly can. Animals that are grown and fed naturally, and allowed to roam freely will always give better tasting meat. It will be denser with a good marbling of fat and have a deeper flavor. It will also retain less water and shrink less when cooked. Some meats benefit from being aged; beef is more often available dry-aged these days, which is actually a return to older practice and gives much better, more intense flavors. Some game birds also benefit from being aged—known as "hanging" in their case—but always ask the advice of a butcher regarding hung game before buying, and tell him or her what you intend to use it for. Other than these, it's always best to buy the freshest meat possible.

Good pork is recognizable by its flesh being dense (animals that have been grown fast, using hormones, will have softer, looser meat with a wider grain). It should be pink, instead of brown or gray, and should be finely marbled with white fat. Pork is rich in nutrients but its fat content is twice as high as that of beef. Pork can be eaten hot or cold, but never raw. The most tender part of the pig is the loin, which is used for chops, roasts, and tenderloins (fillets). If you can, try to use pancetta when it's called for in a recipe, but if you can't find it, you can easily substitute it with unsmoked bacon.

High-quality, organically raised beef is getting easier to find these days. Good meat that has been aged before being packaged tends to be dark red with creamy yellow fat. If the meat has been vacuum-packed shortly after slaughter it will be a brighter red with white fat. Rare breeds hung for a long time will be more expensive, but more flavorsome. Beef has a high nutritional value but it is also higher in cholesterol than veal. Always ask your butcher for humanely reared veal, or read the packaging—it should be grass-fed or free-range. When slaughtered between four and six months, the meat is rose-colored, tender, has a high water content, and is low in fat. The fat is white with shades of pink. Good veal should be very soft, tender, and pale in color—from white to pink.

Lamb is usually six to eight months old in the United States, and no older than a year, and up to a year old in the UK. It will be young and mild enough in flavor to be used in any Italian recipe. In the UK, sheep more than a year old, but less than two years old is called hogget. Mutton is more than a year old in the United States and is richer and gamier and needs longer cooking. It's at least two years old in the UK. Sheep are very fatty, so their meat will shrink as the fat melts and the muscles contract when you cook, so buy more than you think you need.

Game is leaner than most livestock and lends itself beautifully to slow cooking and seasonal flavors, making for rich, unctuous wintry stews. Young game works well for roasting and frying, older animals are better for stewing and braising. With pinkish white, tender meat that is rich in protein and low in fats, rabbit is very easily digested and contains almost no cholesterol. If you're lucky enough to be eating shot game, look for shot when you are prepping, carving, and, especially, eating it!

In terms of poultry, vast amounts of chicken are intensively reared. Avoid them if you can. Cage-free (free-range or free-roaming) and organic birds are well worth the money for their superior flavor and texture. You can tell a good chicken by its skin, which should be velvety and pale. Turkeys are also intensively reared—if so, they can give disappointingly flavorless meat. Splash out on a cage-free bird—rare breeds have the best flavors of all, because they have not been bred for size alone.

Geese are best bought in season and fresh rather than frozen. They can be very large, so if you will be cooking it in a conventional domestic oven, it would be best to buy one that's about 6½ lb (3 kg), which will be about eight to nine months old. It's best to buy guinea fowl that are seven to ten months old—if a bird is older than that, it'll need to be a hung bird, which will taste far stronger.

Storage

Beef and pork can be stored in the refrigerator at 32–39°F/0–4°C for three to six days, whereas poultry should be stored for only three to four days. Ground (minced) meat and sausages should be consumed within a day. Once cooked, these can be kept in the refrigerator for three to four days. Storing meat in appropriate containers or wrapped in plastic wrap (clingfilm) is essential to preserve its natural water content. Otherwise, the meat will harden and its taste will change. Protecting meat also helps to prevent meat oxidation, which will cause it to turn from red to gray as well as alter its flavor. Both raw and cooked meat can be frozen for periods ranging from a month to up to a year. Beef can be stored in the freezer for up to a year but poultry and pork should not be kept for more than a few months. It is important to allow the meat to defrost slowly before it is cooked.

How to use this book

Recipes from an Italian Butcher is divided into chapters according to the main types of meat. Each chapter opens with an explanation of the different cuts for that particular type of meat, which cooking methods those cuts are most suited to, and descriptions of how to choose and prepare them. There is advice on what to ask your butcher and illustrations of the relevant animal, showing the Italian, American, and British cuts. This practical information is followed by a collection of delicious, simple, and authentic Italian recipes for each kind of meat.

Kitchen Utensils

Before you start cooking, meat needs to be prepared by following a few important rules. It should be cut in the correct places, then diced, pounded, or trussed—and, of course, you will also need the correct pot or pan for the right cooking method.

Cutting (chopping) boards

You will need one for raw food and one for cooked. Plastic boards are hardwearing and easier to clean. If you prefer to use wooden boards, be sure to choose a good-quality wood. Don't leave it soaking in water, or the wood may split.

Dutch oven (casserole)

A dish made of cast iron or earthenware, deep and with a lid for slow and prolonged cooking. These heavy, sturdy pots conduct heat well, which means meat gets browned evenly. It is highly recommended for tender, delicate meats (poultry and white meat) or very lean meats that are first basted with lard or similar. They can be used on the stove (hob) and in an oven and come in sizes large enough to hold whole pieces of meat, game, and poultry.

Kitchen twine

This is not essential kitchen equipment but it is extremely useful and inexpensive. Made of plain, unbleached cotton, it can be used to hold together roasts, secure a rolled, stuffed piece of meat, or truss the perfect chicken or turkey.

Knives

For home cooking, you will need one knife with a long, hard, and sharp blade for raw meat, as well as another one with a long, flexible, serrated blade for slicing cooked meat. Before cutting the meat—whether raw or already cooked—it is advisable to place it on a cutting (chopping) board and hold it securely in place with a carving fork. Meat must always be cut against the grain.

A meat tenderizer

Many recipes require meat to be pounded. Tenderizing meat with a meat mallet softens the fibers, making the meat easier to digest.

Poultry shears

These shears can be used before or after cooking to cut poultry or rabbit into smaller pieces when it has been bought as a whole or in larger cuts.

Roasting pans

Choose the sturdiest roasting pans you can find, as thin pans can warp when used directly on the stove (hob) or in the oven at high temperatures. You will need a large, deep one with fairly tall sides. A small one is also useful for smaller pieces of meat, because the juices will evaporate less.

Stove-to-oven pan

Perhaps the most useful pan of all, a large pan that can go on the stove (hob) and into the oven. Make sure the handles are ovenproof. A nonstick interior is helpful but not essential. Be extra careful with cast-iron pans because the metal conducts heat quickly and stays hot for a long time.

Tongs and thermometer

Tongs can be used to turn over pieces of meat during cooking, while a thermometer can be used to check the internal temperature of roasted meat by inserting it directly into the meat. However, pricking the meat during cooking is not recommended, because it can cause the juices to run out.

Trussing needle

A needle used for trussing (tying) poultry, such as chicken, duck, or turkey, for cooking. This is done to ensure the bird keeps its shape and cooks evenly. It can also be used to sew the stuffed cavity of a bird closed. They are typically about 8 inches/20 cm long.

Pork

Italian food is all but unimaginable without *maiale*. Porchetta is the most famous of Italian pork dishes, a boneless, stuffed, rolled roast that originated in central Italy, and is often sold by the slice, sometimes in bread rolls, but is just as popular as a homecooked meal. In Italy no part of the pig is ever thrown away—everything can be successfully transformed into tasty and nutritious foods that add flavor to many dishes. Italian ingenuity and economy with the pig can be seen in *guanciale*, cured pig cheek, the finest bacon you'll ever eat! And even when things are kept simple, such as with Roasted Pork Loin (see page 24) or stewed pork shoulder (see page 38), it is delicious and full of flavor.

The majority of the pork raised in Italy now comes from breeds that aren't originally Italian. As in the United States, lean pork is popular in Italy and fattier breeds are far less frequently found. Today, rare breeds of pig are more widely available in the United States, and often have better flavor, but good pork is good pork, and good fresh pork is recognizable by its flesh being dense (animals that have been grown fast, using hormones, will have softer, looser meat with a wider grain). It should be pink, instead of brown or gray, and should be finely marbled with white fat. It works well with sage and rosemary and Tuscan or cannellini (white kidney) beans. Use pancetta in recipes when it's asked for, if you can, but if you can't, use unsmoked bacon.

To get good, crisp skin (crackling) on roasted pork, make sure the skin is dry before cooking. You can do this by leaving it in the refrigerator, uncovered, for a few hours. Then take it out of the refrigerator and let it come up to room temperature before cooking. Before putting the meat in the oven, score the fat with the sharpest blade you have, without going right through to the meat, and make the cuts about ½ inch/1 cm apart. Salt the skin immediately before putting it in the oven. Put in the oven at the highest temperature possible for the first 20 minutes.

Pork requires much longer cooking times—about 25 minutes per 1 lb 2 oz/500 g.

Roasting cuts

It's easier to carve pork when it's off the bone, so ask the butcher to remove it from joints where possible, unless the recipe asks for it to be bone-in.

Shoulder, blade, and hand (arm shoulder) are all good, relatively inexpensive, with great flavor, and can be stuffed. Loin is more expensive and can be difficult to carve, but if you have the time to put in the effort, it's worth it. Loin should be roasted in a preheated low-to-medium oven so that the heat can penetrate to the center before a crust forms on the outside. The most commonly used cut is leg—it's great for a large group but its leanness means it dries out easily. A fattier, very flavorsome cut is the side (belly)—make sure the skin is scored before roasting to get great crackling and a great flavor. Tenderloin (fillet) and the top part of the leg (chump) are also fattier and moister than leg and work well if rolled.

Stewing and Braising Cuts

Pork is great for stewing and braising—it is perfectly suited to slow cooking and keeps its flavor. Drier cuts, such as leg and loin, really benefit from extra cooking time and make great stews or casseroles. Slow-cooking fattier pork side (belly) also works really well, you just need to make sure to skim off any excess fat that rises to the surface at the end of the cooking time.

Italian cuts and cooking techniques

1 Lonza
Ideal for roasting

2 Cosciotto
The part used
to make ham

3 Piedini
Boiling and frying

4 Puntine costine
Stewing and
braising

5 Pancetta, guanciale
For forcemeats
or for larding
and wrapping
dry meats

6 Filetto, lombo
Recommended for
roasting and grilling

7 Carré
Extremely tasty
chops

8 Spalla
For roasting
and stewing

9 Testa
Boiling

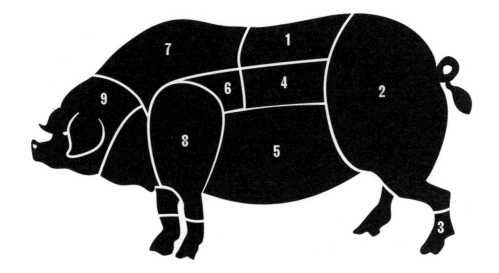

American cuts and cooking techniques

1 Head
Head cheese (brawn)

2 Blade shoulder
Roasting and braising, plus cutting into chops for broiling (grilling) or frying, and slicing for stir-frying

3 Loin
Roasting and cut into tenderloin for roasting, into medallions for frying, and into chops for broiling (grilling)

4 Leg
Roasting and cut into chops for boiling and braising

5 Side
Stuffing and roasting, ground (minced) for terrines, cut into spareribs, and adds flavor to casseroles

6 Arm shoulder
Braising

7 Hock
Braising

8 Foot
Braising

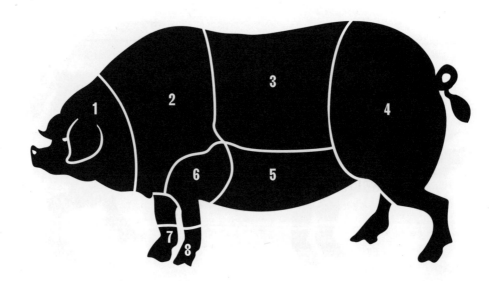

British cuts and cooking techniques

1 Head
Head cheese
(brawn) and
pet food

2 Spare rib
Cut into chops
for broiling (grilling)
or frying, sliced
for stir-fries

3 Blade
Roasting and
braising

4 Loin
Roasting, cut
into fillets for
roasting, frying,
and medallions
and into chops for
broiling (grilling)

**5 Chump and leg
(fillet end)**
Roasting, cut into
chops for broiling
(grilling) and
braising

6 Leg (knuckle end)
Roasting

7 Hock
Roasting

8 Belly (flank)
Stuffing
and roasting,
ground (minced)
for terrines,
spare-ribs, adds
flavor to casseroles

9 Hand
Braising

10 Trotter
Braising

Arista al forno

Roasted Pork Loin

Serves 4
Preparation: 20 minutes
Cooking: 1 hour, plus
   10 minutes resting

1 clove garlic, central core
   removed
1 sprig rosemary
1 lb 8½ oz/700 g pork loin
3½ oz/100 g pancetta slices
2–3 tablespoons extra virgin
   olive oil
⅔ cup (5 fl oz/150 ml) dry
   white wine
salt and pepper

Preheat the oven to 350°F/180°C/Gas Mark 4. Chop the garlic and rosemary finely. Using a knife, make several deep incisions in the pork and fill the slashes with the chopped ingredients. Rub the meat with a pinch of salt and some pepper, then wrap it in the pancetta and tie it securely with kitchen twine. Put the meat into a roasting pan, drizzle with the olive oil, and cook in the oven for 20 minutes. Pour the white wine around the meat and then cook for another 40 minutes.

Place the meat on a cutting (chopping) board, remove the kitchen twine, wrap in kitchen foil, and let rest for 10 minutes. This will allow the cooking juices to be reabsorbed into the meat. Carve the meat into slices and reassemble it in a serving dish before serving it with its cooking juices.

Note: This dish is also excellent when served cold with its warmed cooking juices.

Arista all'arancia

Roasted Pork with Orange

Serves 6
Preparation: 15 minutes
Cooking: 1½ hours

3 tablespoons butter
1½ cups (12 fl oz/350 ml) orange
   juice, strained
1 teaspoon orange zest
1 clove garlic
pinch of chili powder
pinch of dried oregano
1 x 2¼-lb/1-kg pork loin, boned
salt and pepper

Photograph opposite

Preheat the oven to 350°F/180°C/Gas Mark 4. Melt the butter in a saucepan, add the orange juice, zest, garlic, chili powder, and oregano, season with salt and pepper, and mix well. Rub the meat with salt and pepper and place in a roasting pan. Pour in the orange mixture and roast, basting frequently, for about 1½ hours, or until tender. Carve into slices and serve with the cooking juices.

Lonza di maiale al ginepro

Pork Loin with Juniper Berries

Serves 4
Preparation: 20 minutes,
plus 2 hours marinating
Cooking: 1 hour 20 minutes,
plus 5 minutes resting

1¾ lb/800 g pork loin
1 shallot, sliced
1 onion, chopped
10 juniper berries, crushed
2 bay leaves
½ cup (4 fl oz/120 ml) dry
    white wine
4–6 tablespoons olive oil
3½ oz/100 g pancetta slices
salt and pepper

Using a sharp knife, make several cuts in the loin and insert the sliced shallot. Put the chopped onion into a bowl and add the crushed juniper berries, the bay leaves, wine, 2–3 tablespoons of the oil, and salt and pepper. Place the meat on top of this mixture and marinate for 2 hours in the refrigerator.

Preheat the oven to 350°F/180°C/Gas Mark 4. Drain the meat, reserving the marinade. Wrap the pork in the pancetta and tie it with kitchen twine. Pour the remaining oil into a roasting pan, place the pork loin in the pan, and roast in the oven for 1 hour 20 minutes, basting it occasionally with a tablespoon of the marinade. Remove from the oven and cut off the kitchen twine. Rest for 5 minutes, then thinly slice the loin and place on a serving platter. Serve drizzled with the warm cooking juices.

Note: Pancetta can easily be replaced with slices of lard. If you choose to use lard, the meat should be cooked without oil.

Carré con purè di zucca e patate

Pork Loin with Mashed Pumpkin and Potato

Serves 6
Preparation: 30 minutes
Cooking: 1½ hours

olive oil, for oiling
1 x 2½ -lb/1.2-kg pork loin
few sage leaves
1 sprig rosemary
⅔ cup (5 fl oz/150 ml) dry
   white wine
1¾ lb/800 g pumpkin, peeled,
   seeded, and diced
1 lb 2 oz/500 g potatoes,
   peeled and chopped
4 tablespoons butter
3½ oz/100 g shallots, chopped
splash of red wine vinegar
salt and pepper

Preheat the oven to 400°F/200°C/Gas Mark 6 and oil a roasting pan. Season the pork with salt and pepper and place in the prepared pan. Add the sage and rosemary and roast the pork in the oven for 20 minutes, basting with wine occasionally.

After the meat has been roasting for 20 minutes, place the diced pumpkin into another roasting pan, drizzle with a little oil, season, and cover with foil. Place in the oven alongside the pork. Reduce the oven temperature to 350°F/180°C/Gas Mark 4 and roast both the squash and pork for 40 minutes, basting the pork with wine occasionally. Add a little water if the pan dries out. Remove from the oven and keep warm.

Bring a pan of water to a boil, add the potatoes, and boil for about 20 minutes, or until tender, then drain and return to the pan. When the pumpkin is ready, remove from the oven, add to the still hot potatoes, and mash with a potato masher, adding a pinch of salt and half the butter. Keep warm.

Melt the remaining butter in a saucepan, add the chopped shallots and the vinegar, and let the vinegar evaporate. Gently cook the shallots, basting them with some of the meat cooking juices until tender. Be careful not to let them dry out or burn; they just need to soften and cook through. Cut the pork into slices, place in a serving dish with the shallots on one side and the mashed pumpkin and potato on the other.

Note: When you cook the shallots, check them regularly, because they tend to burn easily. If needed, add a ladleful of broth (stock) or hot water.

Maiale in cartoccio al forno

Pork Tenderloin Baked in Foil

Serves 4
Preparation: 15 minutes
Cooking: 50 minutes, plus
   5 minutes resting

1 lb 5 oz/600 g pork tenderloin
   (fillet)
1 oz/30 g pancetta in one single
   slice, cut into matchsticks
3 tablespoons olive oil, plus extra
   for brushing
1 onion, cut into very thin strips
2 carrots, cut into very thin strips
salt and pepper

Preheat the oven to 350°F/180°C/Gas Mark 4. Rub the meat with a pinch of salt and some pepper. Using a sharp knife, make 10 cuts in the meat and insert the pancetta sticks. In a hot skillet (frying pan), heat the oil and seal the meat all over.

Spread a large rectangular piece of kitchen foil on a work surface, brush with some oil, and place the meat on top with the onion and the carrots strips. Season with salt and pepper and wrap the foil around the meat, making a package. Put onto a baking sheet and cook in the oven for 40–45 minutes.

Open the package and if the meat and the vegetables are too moist, leave the foil open and cook for another 5 minutes. When the meat is ready, let it rest for 5 minutes before slicing it and serving with the vegetables.

Carré di maiale al forno con patate

Roasted Pork Loin with Potatoes

Serves 6
Preparation: 30 minutes
Cooking: 1¼ hours

2½ lb/1.2 kg bone-in pork loin
   prepared by your butcher
1½ oz/40 g smoked pancetta
   in a single piece, cut into
   matchsticks
4–5 tablespoons extra virgin
   olive oil
⅔ cup (5 fl oz/150 ml) white wine
1¾ lb/800 g potatoes, peeled and
   cut into small pieces
1 sprig rosemary
salt and pepper

Photograph opposite

Preheat the oven to 400°F/200°C/Gas Mark 6. Rub the meat with a pinch of salt and some pepper. Using a sharp knife, make several incisions in the meat, and insert a stick of pancetta into each one. Put the meat into a roasting pan with the olive oil and brown it in the oven for 20 minutes. Remove the pan from the oven, pour the white wine around the meat, and cook for another 30 minutes.

Meanwhile, bring a pan of water to a boil, add the potatoes, and parboil in the boiling water for 10 minutes. Drain and add to the meat along with the rosemary sprig and a pinch of salt. Reduce the oven temperature to 350°F/180°C/Gas Mark 4 and cook the meat and potatoes for another 30–35 minutes.

Note: Before placing the meat in the oven, wrap the bones of the pork loin in foil so that they don't turn dark brown during cooking.

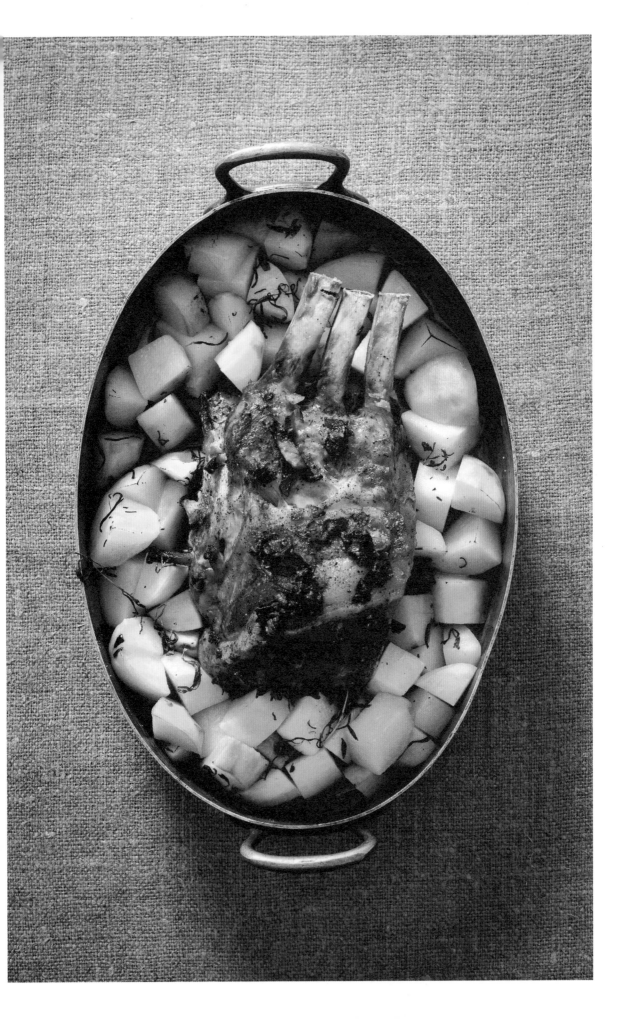

Arrosto di maiale al sidro e mele

Roasted Pork Loin with Apples and Cider

Serves 6
Preparation: 15 minutes
Cooking: 1¼ hours, plus
   15 minutes resting

1 x 1¾-lb/800-g pork loin
sweet salt from Cervia with
   aromatic herbs, to rub
2 sprigs rosemary
2 tablespoons butter
4 tablespoons extra virgin olive oil
4 small apples
2 sprigs sage
1 clove garlic, crushed
1¼ cups (10 fl oz/300 ml) hard
   apple cider
pepper

Rub the pork loin with the sweet salt and some pepper. Tie the meat with kitchen twine, sticking the rosemary under the twine. Heat the butter and oil in a flameproof Dutch oven (casserole) over high heat, add the meat, and sear, turning frequently without piercing, until it is browned all over.

Meanwhile, wash the apples, dry them, and make an incision with a sharp knife all the way around the circumference, ¾–1¼ inches/ 2–3 cm from the bottom. Set aside.

When the meat is browned all over, add the sage and crushed garlic to the Dutch oven, reduce the heat, pour in the cider, and simmer until reduced. Add the apples, cover, and reduce the heat to low. Cook for 50–60 minutes, turning the pork occasionally, again without piercing the meat. Remove the meat from the Dutch oven, cover, and rest for 15 minutes. Cut off the kitchen twine and carve the meat into slices. Strain the cooking juices and transfer to a gravy boat. Serve the roasted pork with the apples, spooning over the cooking juices.

Note: Sweet salt from Cervia is a raw sea salt that has not been artificially dried and still preserves its natural humidity. Its sweetness makes it ideal for cooking. It can be combined with aromatic herbs from Romagna: chives, garlic, thyme, and chili pepper.

Maiale al latte

Pork Tenderloin Braised in Milk

Serves 6
Preparation: 15 minutes, plus
   12 hours marinating
Cooking: 1½ hours, plus
   15 minutes resting

2½ lb/1.2 kg pork tenderloin
   (fillet)
4 peppercorns
6¼ cups (50 fl oz/1.5 liters)
   whole milk
2 cloves garlic, grated
5 oz/150 g pancetta, in thin slices
4 tablespoons olive oil
beef broth (stock), for drizzling
salt
spinach cooked in butter,
   sprinkled with croutons,
   to serve

Put the meat into a large bowl with the peppercorns and milk, then cover with plastic wrap (clingfilm) and marinate in the refrigerator for 12 hours. Drain the meat and pat dry.

Preheat the oven to 350°F/180°C/Gas Mark 4. Rub the meat with the grated garlic and a little salt, then wrap in the pancetta slices and secure with kitchen twine. Put the meat into a roasting pan, drizzle with the oil and some beef broth (stock), and cook in the oven for 1½ hours, basting the meat occasionally with the cooking juices. Keep adding broth so that the pan does not dry out. Once cooked, remove the kitchen twine and pancetta. Wrap the meat in parchment paper and rest for at least 15 minutes.

Meanwhile, strain the cooking juices and pour into a small pan. Heat gently until the juices have thickened slightly, then remove from the heat. Cut the meat into thin slices, place on a serving platter, spoon over the thickened cooking juices, and serve with spinach cooked in butter and sprinkled with croutons.

Note: An alternative method is to sear the meat on the stove (hob), add some sliced shallots, and let brown. Dust with all-purpose (plain) flour and cook, adding 3 cups (25 fl oz/750 ml) milk, little by little, for about 1½ hours.

Stinco di maiale arrosto al miele e senape

Roasted Pork Shank with Honey and Mustard

Serves 6
Preparation: 10 minutes
Cooking: 3 hours, plus
 10 minutes resting

3 tablespoons grainy Dijon mustard
2 tablespoons acacia honey
3 pork shanks
3 tablespoons butter
scant 1 cup (7 fl oz/200 ml)
 white wine
3 sprigs tarragon, leaves only,
 chopped
½ green (white) cabbage, cored
 and very finely sliced
salt

Photograph opposite

Preheat the oven to 400°F/200°F/Gas Mark 6. Mix the mustard and honey together in a small bowl. Season the pork shanks with salt and brush with the mustard mixture.

Melt the butter in a roasting pan over medium heat, add the pork shanks, white wine, and half the chopped tarragon. Transfer the pan to the oven and cook for about 3 hours, basting frequently with the cooking juices, until tender.

Remove the pork shanks from the oven, cover with kitchen foil, and rest for 10 minutes. Sprinkle the remaining tarragon over the meat and serve with the sliced cabbage dressed with the cooking juices.

Note: Smoked pork shanks, which are usually precooked, can also be used for this recipe. The meat should be boiled in water for 1 hour and then roasted in an oven preheated to 350°F/180°C/ Gas Mark 4 for another hour.

Filetti di maiale al sale di agrumi e mirto

Pork Tenderloins in Citrus-and-Myrtle Scented Salt

Serves 4
Preparation: 20 minutes
Cooking: 55 minutes

2 oranges, washed, dried, and zest
    coarsely grated
2 unwaxed lemons, washed, dried,
    and zest coarsely grated
about 10 cups (4½ lb/2 kg) kosher
    or coarse salt
2 egg whites
4 sprigs myrtle, leaves only
2 pork tenderloins (fillets)

For the sauce
3 tablespoons (2 oz/50 g) bitter
    orange marmalade
¼ cup (2 fl oz/60 ml) rum
1½ tablespoons butter
1 sprig myrtle
black pepper

Photograph opposite

Preheat the oven to 350°F/180°C/Gas Mark 4. Mix the orange and lemon zest with the kosher or coarse salt, egg whites, and myrtle leaves together in a bowl. Cover the bottom of a roasting pan with a layer of the orange-scented salt. Place the pork tenderloins (fillets) in the center, then cover the meat with the remaining salt. Cook in the oven for 50 minutes.

To make the sauce, mix the marmalade and rum together in a small pan. Add small pats (knobs) of the butter, a generous grind of pepper, and the myrtle sprigs, and cook over low heat for 5–6 minutes.

Break the salt crust covering the meat and remove the meat. Cut into thick slices and serve with the orange sauce.

Note: If you don't like the combination of meat with sweet flavors, replace the orange sauce with ⅔ cup (5 oz/150 g) of plain yogurt or sour cream mixed with 2 teaspoons horseradish paste. Serve with broiled (grilled) radicchio.

Carré al prugne

Rack of Pork with Dried Plums

Serves 6
Preparation: 25 minutes
Cooking: 1½ hours, plus 10 minutes
   resting time

1 x 2¼-lb/1-kg rack of pork,
   chine bone removed and
   ribs uncovered
⅔ cup (5 oz/150 g) dried plums
   (prunes), pitted
4 tablespoons butter
2 tablespoons olive oil
1 shallot, chopped
2 tablespoons brandy
salt and pepper

Preheat the oven to 400°F/200°C/Gas Mark 6. Open out the pork like a book and arrange a row of dried plums (prunes) along the meat. Chop the remaining dried plums and set aside. Roll the pork and tie with kitchen twine passed between the ribs, then season.

Heat half the butter and the oil in a roasting pan, then remove from the heat, add the pork, and roast in the oven, basting occasionally, for 1¼ hours.

To make the sauce, melt the remaining butter in a skillet (frying pan), add the chopped shallot, and cook over low heat for 5 minutes. Add the chopped dried plums and cook for 5 minutes. Pour in the brandy and ignite.

Remove the meat from the roasting pan and let rest for 10 minutes. Skim off the fat from the cooking juices and strain the juices into the dried plum (prune) sauce. Untie the meat and carve it into slices. Serve with the dried plum sauce.

Spezzatino con piselli

Pork Stew with Peas

Serves 4
Preparation: 25 minutes
Cooking: 1¼ hours

scant 1 cup (7 oz/200 g) canned
   tomatoes
3 tablespoons butter
2 tablespoons olive oil
1 onion, chopped
1 clove garlic, chopped
1 lb 5 oz/600 g boneless pork
   shoulder, cut into cubes
¾ cup (6 fl oz/175 ml) red wine
2¼ lb/1 kg fresh peas, shelled
salt and pepper

Photograph opposite

Pour the tomatoes with their juices into a food processor and process to a purée. Heat the butter and oil in a large pan, add the onion and garlic, and cook over low heat, stirring occasionally, for 5 minutes. Add the pork and cook, stirring frequently, until lightly browned all over, then season with salt and pepper. Pour in the wine and cook until it has evaporated, then add the puréed tomatoes and the peas. Simmer gently for 1 hour. Transfer the stew to a warm serving dish.

Spezzatino speziato

Spicy Pork Stew

Serves 6
Preparation: 20 minutes
Cooking: 55 minutes

4 tablespoons butter
2¼ lb/1 kg boneless pork shoulder,
   cut into cubes
1½ cups (12 fl oz/350 ml) dry
   white wine
1 teaspoon ground cumin
1 clove garlic, chopped
5 lemon slices, chopped
2 teaspoons ground coriander
salt and pepper
herbs of your choice, to garnish

Photograph opposite

Melt the butter in a large saucepan, add the pork, and cook over high heat, stirring frequently, until browned all over. Pour in half the wine, add the cumin and garlic, and season with salt and plenty of pepper. Mix well and bring to a boil, then cover, lower the heat, and simmer for 30 minutes, or until tender. Pour in the remaining wine and add the lemon. Increase the heat to medium and cook, stirring continuously, until thickened. Stir in the coriander, garnish with herbs of your choice, and serve.

Brasato di capocollo

Braised Pork

Serves 4
Preparation: 20 minutes, plus
   8 hours marinating
Cooking: 1½ hours

1 x 1¾ lb/800 g capocollo pork loin
2 tablespoons olive oil
pat (knob) of butter
1¼ cups (10 fl oz/300 ml) Merlot
3–4 tablespoons puréed canned
   tomatoes (passata)
meat broth (stock), to cover
salt
Polenta (page 285) or Creamy
   Mashed Potatoes (page 281)
   with truffle shavings, to serve

For the marinade:
1¼ cups (10 fl oz/300 ml) Merlot
1 onion, coarsely chopped
2 bay leaves
4 juniper berries
8 black peppercorns
4 cloves

Cut the pork into cubes and put into a large nonreactive dish, pour in the wine, onion, and spices, cover with plastic wrap (clingfilm), and marinate in the refrigerator for 8 hours or overnight.

When you are ready to cook, remove the meat from the marinade, strain the marinade, keeping the onions and spices separate from the liquid, and set aside. Heat the oil and butter in a large—but not too deep—flameproof Dutch oven (casserole), add the meat, and sear over medium heat. Do this in batches if necessary. Let the water from the meat evaporate completely.

When all the meat has browned, return it to the Dutch oven, season with salt, and pour in the strained marinade along with the rest of the wine to cover the meat. Add the puréed canned tomatoes (passata) and let the wine evaporate completely. Add the onions reserved from the marinade and pour in the broth (stock) until it just covers the meat. Reduce the heat and cook for 30 minutes, or until the meat and vegetables are tender, checking regularly and adding a little water if needed.

Serve the braised pork with polenta or creamy mashed potatoes with truffle shavings.

Arrosto con il rosmarino

Braised Pork with Rosemary

Serves 6
Preparation: 20 minutes, plus
   10 minutes resting
Cooking: 1¾ hours

needles from 1–2 sprigs rosemary
1 x 2¼-lb/1-kg pork loin pork,
   boned
2 tablespoons butter
6 tablespoons olive oil
1 clove garlic, crushed
½ onion, chopped
¾ cup (6 fl oz/175 ml) dry
   white wine
1 tablespoon white wine vinegar
1 teaspoon Dijon mustard
salt and pepper

Photograph opposite

Push half the rosemary needles into the meat and tie neatly with kitchen twine. Heat the butter and 4 tablespoons of the oil in a large pan, add the pork, and cook, turning frequently, until golden brown all over. Add the garlic, onion, and remaining rosemary, then pour in the wine and cook until evaporated. Season, cover, and simmer for about 1½ hours, or until tender. Remove the pork from the pan and let rest for 10 minutes.

Meanwhile, stir the vinegar, the remaining oil, the mustard, and a pinch of pepper into the cooking juices. Pour the sauce into a sauceboat.

Remove the kitchen twine from the pork, carve the meat into fairly thick slices, and place in a warm serving dish. Pour the sauce over the meat and serve.

Arista con salsa alle albicocche

Pork Loin with Apricot Sauce

Serves 6
Preparation: 25 minutes, plus
   8 hours marinating
Cooking: 1½ hours

3½ lb/1.6 kg pork loin, deboned
   and bones set aside
1¼ cups (10 fl oz/300 ml) grappa
1⅓ cup (8 oz/225 g) dried apricots
1 tablespoon olive oil
broth (stock), as needed (optional)
5 tablespoons white wine vinegar
2 tablespoons mustard
2 tablespoons superfine (caster)
   sugar
2 tablespoons all-purpose
   (plain) flour
1 tablespoon butter
salt and pepper
herbs of your choice, to garnish

For the marinade:
1 bottle (25 fl oz/750 ml) dry
   white wine
5 cloves
3 cloves garlic, chopped
1 onion, chopped
30 black peppercorns
kosher or coarse salt

Photograph opposite

Mix all the ingredients for the marinade together in a large bowl. Put the meat and bones into the marinade, cover, and let marinate in the refrigerator for 8 hours or overnight.

Pour the grappa into a bowl, add the dried apricots, and let soften for 5 hours.

The next day, drain the pork loin and bones, strain the marinade, and set aside. Heat the oil in a Dutch oven (casserole) over medium heat, add the drained pork loin and bones, and cook for about 5 minutes, or until they are browned all over. Pour in the strained marinade, season with salt and pepper, and bring to a boil. Reduce the heat, cover, and cook for 1 hour, turning the meat occasionally. Remove the meat from the Dutch oven, cover with kitchen foil, and keep in a warm place.

Meanwhile, strain the cooking juices. You should have about 1½ cups (12 fl oz/350 ml) of liquid. Add some broth (stock) if necessary. Pour the liquid into the Dutch oven, add the apricots, grappa, vinegar, mustard, and sugar, and place over low heat for 30 minutes. Mix the flour and butter together in a bowl, add to the sauce, and cook for 2 minutes, or until thickened slightly.

Serve the meat cut into slices with the warm sauce and garnish with herbs of your choice.

Bocconcini ai capperi

Pork with Capers

Serves 4
Preparation: 15 minutes
Cooking: 1 hour 40 minutes

3 tablespoons butter
2 tablespoons olive oil
1 x 1¾-lb/800-g pork loin,
    cut into cubes
1 onion, chopped
1 stalk celery, chopped
3 sage leaves, chopped
pinch of thyme
1 bay leaf
scant 1 cup (7 fl oz/200 ml)
    dry white wine
1 tablespoon all-purpose
    (plain) flour, sifted
2 tablespoons capers, rinsed
2 pickles (gherkins), sliced
1 egg yolk
salt and pepper

Photograph opposite

Heat the butter and oil in a flameproof Dutch oven (casserole) over high heat. Add the pork and cook for 10 minutes, stirring continuously. Season with salt and pepper and add the onion, celery, sage, thyme, and bay leaf. Reduce the heat to medium, pour in the wine, and let evaporate. Add the sifted flour, mix well, then pour in scant ½ cup (3½ fl oz/100 ml) water. Cover with a lid and let simmer for 1 hour 20 minutes.

Remove the meat from the Dutch oven and set aside. Add the capers and sliced pickles (gherkins) to the Dutch oven, stir, then remove from the heat and stir in the egg yolk. Return the meat to the Dutch oven to let it absorb the flavor of the sauce. Arrange in a serving dish and serve.

Arista al latte profumato

Pork Loin Braised in Infused Milk

Serves 6
Preparation: 20 minutes, plus 12 hours soaking
Cooking: 2 hours 10 minutes

2½ lb/1.2 kg boneless pork loin
8½ cups (88 fl oz/2.5 liters) milk
3 tablespoons butter
2 bay leaves
1 bouillon (stock) cube
pinch of nutmeg
1 sprig thyme, leaves only
salt and pepper

Put the meat into a large bowl, pour in 4¼ cups (34 fl oz/1 liter) milk, and soak in the refrigerator for 12 hours.

Melt the butter in a heavy roasting pan (preferably the same size as the meat) over medium-high heat. Drain the meat well, place it in the pan, and sear for about 6 minutes, or until browned on all sides. Season with pepper. Warm the remaining milk in a pan over low heat, then pour into the roasting pan. Add the bay leaves and bouillon (stock) cube and cook over low heat for about 2 hours, or until almost all the liquid has evaporated. Turn the pork regularly.

A few minutes before the cooking time is finished, add a pinch of nutmeg and thyme to the pan, and season with salt. Remove the meat from the pan and let rest for a few minutes. Blend the cooking juices and dilute with some hot water if there is not enough liquid. Cut the pork loin into slices, drizzle with the hot cooking juices, and serve.

Note: The cooking liquid will be runny and contain lumps. To obtain a smooth, creamy sauce, simply process in a food processor or use a handheld blender.

Serves 6–8
Preparation: 10 minutes
Cooking: 30 minutes

scant ½ cup (3½ fl oz/100 ml) vegetable oil
2½ lb/1.2 kg pork, diced
1 cup (7 oz/200 g) pickled chile peppers (chillies), seeded and thinly sliced
salt and pepper

Photograph opposite

Maiale ai peperoncini sott'aceto

Pork and Pickled Chile Peppers

Heat the oil in a flameproof Dutch oven (casserole) over high heat, add the diced pork, and sear for several minutes until golden brown all over. Add the chiles (chillies), sprinkle with hot water, and reduce the heat to medium. Cook for 20–25 minutes. Season with salt and pepper. Transfer the stew to a serving dish and serve while still hot.

Note: For this recipe, use a fattier cut of pork, such as the shoulder, so that the fat melts during cooking and keeps the meat tender.

Pork Shank in Red Wine with Spinach

Serves 4
Preparation: 20 minutes,
plus 7–8 hours marinating
Cooking: 2 hours 10 minutes

2 pork shanks
2¼ cups (17 fl oz/500 ml)
    red wine
1 onion, ½ sliced and ½ finely
    chopped
4 juniper berries, crushed
1 bay leaf, shredded
2 sprigs parsley, leaves finely
    chopped and stems (stalks)
    removed and reserved
1 sprig rosemary
3 sprigs thyme
2 sprigs marjoram
2–3 strips of unwaxed orange
    zest removed with a potato
    peeler
3 tablespoons butter
1 lb 5 oz/600 g spinach, washed
salt

Photograph opposite

Put the pork shanks into a large dish, pour in the wine, and add the sliced onion, crushed juniper berries, shredded bay leaf, parsley stems (stalks), other herbs, and orange zest. Cover with plastic wrap (clingfilm) and marinate in the refrigerator for 7–8 hours, turning the meat occasionally.

When ready to cook, preheat the oven to 350°F/180°C/Gas Mark 4. Remove the pork shanks from the marinade, pat dry with paper towels, then season with salt. Strain the marinade and set aside.

Melt the butter in a flameproof Dutch oven (casserole) over high heat and sear the pork shanks for 5–6 minutes, turning on all sides. Add the finely chopped onion, reduce the heat to medium, and cook for another 2–3 minutes. Pour the marinade around the meat and cook in the oven for 2 hours, basting the meat occasionally with the cooking juices. When the meat is cooked, remove from the Dutch oven, cover with kitchen foil, and rest for 10 minutes.

Meanwhile, bring a pan of water to a boil and blanch the spinach for 2–3 minutes. Drain well. Put the Dutch oven onto the heat with the pork cooking juices, add the spinach, and sauté for a few minutes until wilted. Transfer to a serving dish and place the pork shanks on top of the wilted spinach. Sprinkle with the chopped parsley leaves to serve.

Note: As an alternative, the pork shanks can be marinated in an aromatic white wine. A finely chopped carrot and celery stalk, and ¾-inch/2-cm piece of grated fresh ginger may be added to the sautéed onion.

Beef

Beef is the king of meats. Its tenderness and depth of flavor depends on three things: the age of the animal, the type of food it was raised on, and the length of time it was hung to mature. Get these right and it's a joy. Historic breeds, such as Longhorn, are being reestablished in the United States, so finding good-quality, organically raised beef is getting easier. You can tell a lot about a cut of meat by its color; aged traditionally, the meat tends to be dark red with creamy yellow fat, but if vacuum-packed shortly after slaughter, it will be a brighter red with white fat and less flavorsome. Rare breeds hung for a long time will be more expensive, but they're always worth it, if you can afford it, for the flavor that develops.

The key to maximizing beef's depth of flavor is to retain its juices, so prepare it on a plate instead of a board, from which they would run off, and always salt it after browning. It's best to take it out of the refrigerator about an hour before cooking, because it will cook better from room temperature—keep it covered and somewhere cool.

The best roasting technique for beef is spit-roasting. The fierce heat causes a light protective layer to form around the meat, which helps retain the juice and intensifies the flavor. Pot roasts can be cooked in the oven or on the stove (hob). They must, in any case, be cooked briefly on the stove to brown and sear the meat to retain the juice. After this, salt is added and the Dutch oven (casserole) is put into a preheated oven. To prevent meat from drying out, baste occasionally with its cooking juices. Medium and large pieces of meat cook better if they are compact. That is why these recipes suggest tying them neatly with kitchen twine.

For braising beef, after browning and moistening it with water or wine, the meat is cooked over low heat for a long time in a flameproof pot with a heavy lid. A few vegetables and herbs or spices are normally also added to the pot, such as onions, carrots, celery, and thyme.

Stewing and "*in umido*" are techniques similar to braising, except the latter usually involves adding tomatoes and contains a small quantity of liquid. In *stracotto* stew, the meat is often larded, then lightly browned all over and moistened with wine, broth (stock), or water. The liquid is then kept at a gentle simmer for 3–4 hours. When cooked, the stew will be thickened and rich.

Roasting cuts

Cuts are divided into four main areas: The two forequarters and two hindquarters. The forequarters are leaner and more muscular so require longer cooking to break down the tissue. There are many cuts that can be roasted, but the best include rib (on the bone or boned and rolled), sirloin, top round (top rump), and tenderloin (fillet). These cuts should be sealed quickly, over high heat, and then basted to prevent them from drying out. Roasting on-the-bone will give a deeper flavor, especially if there's a layer of fat to make it more succulent.

Stewing and Braising Cuts

Shin, brisket (from the belly), chuck, and neck (UK) are great for slow-cooking—either stewing or braising. These leaner cuts tend to have more collagen in them, which breaks down through long, slow cooking into meltingly soft gelatin, giving the beef a moist, tender texture and adding viscosity and body to the juices. Brisket also works well in barbecues and can be thought of as the beef equivalent of ever-popular pulled pork.

Steaks

Tenderloin (fillet) steak is the finest cut—it's the part of the cow that does the least work, so it has the least collagen. It's beautifully tender and should be cooked as quickly as possible over high heat to retain moisture and flavor. Like tenderloin, rib-eye comes from an area of the cow that does little work, so it is another good, tender cut. It's often served medium instead of rare, because it has ribbons of fat running through it and an "eye" of fat at the center that needs to be rendered down.

Round steaks (rump) and hanger (onglet) are more everyday steaks; they have great, meaty flavor, if a chewier texture, and are best served rare or slow-cooked.

Italian cuts and cooking techniques

1 Fiocco
Boiling

2 Brione
Stewing and boiling

3 Fusello
Fairly lean.
Stewing, boiling,
roulades, and
cutlets (escalopes)

4 Collo
Boiling and stewing

5 Reale
Boiling and braising

6 Biancostato di reale
Boiling

7 Cappello del prete
Its Italian
name means
priest's hat and
derives from its
slightly triangular
shape. It is soft
and gelatinous.
Braising, stewing,
and boiling

8 Geretto
Boiling, braising,
and stewing

9 Fesone di spalla
Steaks, boiling,
roulades, cutlets,
and scallops
(escalopes)

10 Coste della croce
Boiling

11 Biancostato di croce
Soups

12 Punta di petto
Boiling and stewing

13 Pancia o bamborino
Soups, stews,
and meatballs

14 Biancostato di pancia
Broth (stocks)
and boiling

15 Costata
Rib steak

16 Controfiletto (Lombata)
Steaks and
Florentine steaks

17 Filetto
The most tender
and tastiest cut.
Roasting and
broiling (grilling)

18 Scalfo
Stewing

19 Scamone
A tender tasty cut.
Large roasts

20 Noce
Very tender.
Scallops
(escalopes),
slices, steaks,
and roasting

21 Spinacino
Stuffed roasts

22 Pesce o piccione
Boiling

23 Girello o magatello
Steaks, scallops
(escalopes),
roasting, stewing,
and boiling, and
also raw for
carpaccio

24 Rosa
Steaks and slices

25 Culaccio o scamone
Roasting, boiling,
braising, and
broiling (grilling)

26 Codone
Stewing and boiling

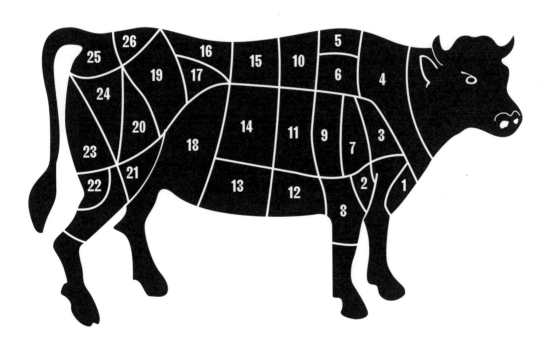

American cuts and cooking techniques

1 Chuck
Braising, pot roasting, and casseroles

2 Flanken-style ribs
Braising, occasionally broiling

3 Rib
Roasting

4 Back rib
Roasting and cut into rib-eye, Delmonico, and Spencer steaks

5 Short loin
Cut into cub, porterhouse, and T-bone steaks

6 Sirloin
Roasting, cut into steaks, tenderloin, and New York strip

7 Round
Cut into boneless rump for roasting, braising, and pot roasting, and round steak, suitable for frying

8 Hind shank
Stewing and making stock

9 Flank
Cut into flank steak rolls, broiling (London broil), and frying

10 Short plate
Braising

11 Brisket
Braising and corned beef

12 Foreshank
Stewing and making broth (stock)

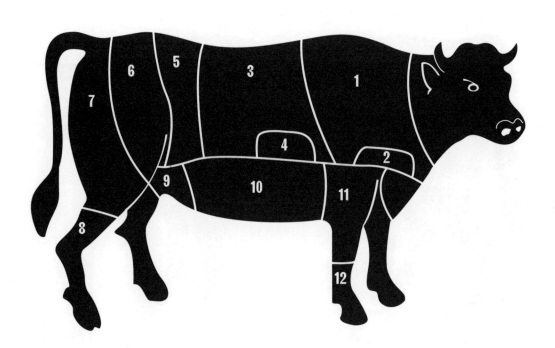

British cuts and cooking techniques

1 Neck
Stewing

2 Clod
Stewing

3 Chuck and blade
Braising and stewing

4 Fore rib
Roasting

5 Thick rib
Roasting

6 Thin rib
Roasting

7 Rolled ribs
Roasting

8 Sirloin
Roasting and cut into steaks and fillets

9 Rump
Roasting and cut into steaks

10 Silverside
Pot-roasting, braising

11 Topside
Braising, pot-roasting

12 Thick flank
Pot-roasting and braising, and slow-frying in slices

13 Leg
Stewing, casseroles

14 Flank
Stewing, and ground (minced) for pies

15 Brisket
Boiling, braising, pot-roasting, and salt beef

16 Shin
Stewing, casseroles

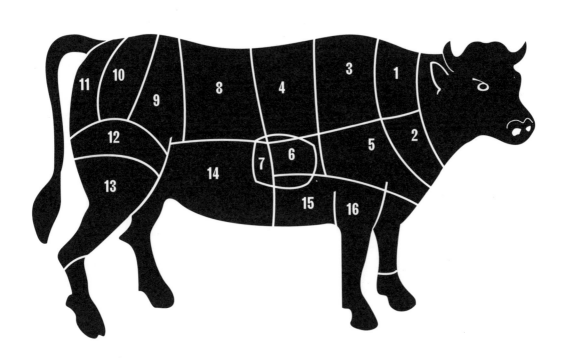

Arrosto in crosta

Roasted Beef in a Pastry Crust

Serves 6
Preparation: 30 minutes, plus
    cooling time
Cooking: 50 minutes

1½ oz/40 g dried porcini
3 tablespoons butter
1 clove garlic, smashed with the
    side of a knife
1 tablespoon chopped parsley
1¾ lb/800 g beef tenderloin (fillet)
½ cup (4 fl oz/120 ml) brandy
3½ oz/100 g prosciutto crudo
8 oz/240 g readymade puff pastry
1 egg yolk, beaten
½ cup (4 fl oz/120 ml) vegetable
    broth (stock)
salt and pepper

Soak the dried mushrooms in a small bowl of lukewarm water for 20 minutes. Drain, remove any residue of soil, and chop finely.

Melt 2 teaspoons of the butter in a Dutch oven (casserole) over medium heat, add the smashed garlic, and fry for a few seconds until browned. Add the chopped mushrooms and a ladleful of boiling water, cover, and cook for 10 minutes. Season with salt and remove the garlic. Add the chopped parsley and turn off the heat.

Season the meat with salt. Melt the remaining butter in another Dutch oven over high heat, add the meat, and sear for 6–7 minutes, turning frequently until browned. Splash the meat with brandy and let it evaporate. Remove the meat from the cooking juices and let cool completely. Set the Dutch oven aside.

Preheat the oven to 400°F/200°C/Gas Mark 6. Cover the cold meat with the mushroom mixture. Lay the prosciutto slices, side by side, slightly overlapping. Place the meat at one end of the prosciutto and roll the meat up in the prosciutto.

Roll the puff pastry out on a flat work surface so it's larger than the meat, then place the rolled-up meat at one end, and roll it in the pastry. Brush the pastry with the beaten egg yolk mixed with a few drops of cold water. (This will give it a shiny, golden crust when cooked.) Cook in the oven for 25 minutes.

Meanwhile, put the Dutch oven with the meat cooking juices over medium heat, pour in the broth (stock), and stir with a wooden spoon to remove all the browned sediment from the bottom of the pan. Once hot, pour into a sauceboat. Serve the beef with the cooking juices.

Manzo all'agrodolce
Sweet-and-Sour Beef

Serves 4
Preparation: 15 minutes
Cooking: 45 minutes

1¾ lb/800 g beef round (topside)
3 tablespoons butter
2 onions, finely chopped
1 cup (6½ oz/180 g) pitted dried
    plums (prunes), cut into
    large pieces
2 tablespoons white wine vinegar
1 bunch parsley, chopped
salt and pepper

Preheat the oven to 350°F/180°C/Gas Mark 4. Tie the meat with kitchen twine and rub it with the butter. Put into a large skillet (frying pan) over high heat and brown the meat all over.

Cover the bottom of a roasting pan with a layer of the chopped onions. Place the browned meat on top, pour over any melted butter left in the skillet, and season with salt and pepper. Cook in the oven for 40 minutes, basting it with hot water occasionally.

Meanwhile, put the dried plums (prunes) into a small pot, pour in ½ cup (4 fl oz/120 ml) water and the vinegar, and cook gently over low heat, until softened. Season with salt and pepper and cook for another 10 minutes. Remove the meat from the oven and rest for 5 minutes.

Process the cooking juices in a food processor or with a handheld blender. Cut the meat into slices, pour over the cooking juices, and sprinkle with the parsley. Serve the dried plum sauce on the side.

Magatello lardellato
Larded Beef

Serves 6
Preparation: 20 minutes, plus
    1 hour freezing
Cooking: 40 minutes

3½ oz/100 g single slice speck,
    cut into matchsticks
6 bay leaves
3 sprigs thyme
1 x 1 lb 8½ oz/700 g beef eye
    of round steak (silverside)
olive oil, for brushing and oiling
⅔ cup (5 fl oz/150 ml) dry
    white wine
scant ½ cup (3½ fl oz/100 ml)
    vegetable broth (stock)
salt and pepper

Freeze the speck matchsticks for 1 hour until they harden. Preheat the oven to 425°F/220°C/Gas Mark 7.

Finely chop 1 bay leaf and 1 sprig of thyme (leaves picked) together, and season with salt and pepper. Roll the speck sticks in the chopped herbs. Using a sharp knife, make several cuts in the beef, then insert the speck sticks and brush with oil. In a hot skillet (frying pan), seal the beef all over, then put into a roasting pan and pour over any juices from the skillet. Tuck in the remaining bay leaves and thyme sprigs and pour in the wine. Cook in the oven for 25 minutes, basting it occasionally with the cooking juices. The meat should be nicely browned but not dry. Check every now and then and if the roasting pan is dry add a little water.

Remove the meat from the pan and let rest for 10 minutes. To collect all the remaining cooking juices, deglaze the roasting pan with the broth (stock) over a medium heat and stir with a wooden spoon to remove all the browned sediment from the bottom of the pan. Reduce slightly and strain. Cut the meat into thin slices and serve with the strained cooking juices.

Roast-beef con le castagne

Roasted Beef with Chestnuts

Serves 6
Preparation: 15 minutes, plus
   6 hours soaking
Cooking: 1–1¼ hours, plus
   10 minutes resting

3½ oz/100 g dried white
   chestnuts
1 x 2¼-lb/1-kg beef tenderloin
   (fillet)
2 tablespoons butter
1 tablespoon olive oil
1 celery stalk, chopped
1 onion, chopped
1 carrot, chopped
1 sprig rosemary, chopped
5 tablespoons dry white wine
3 tablespoons heavy (double)
   cream
salt and pepper
Green Beans with Oil and Garlic
   (page 260), to serve (optional)

Photograph opposite

Soak the chestnuts in a bowl of warm water for 6 hours, then drain.

Preheat the oven to 400°F/200°C/Gas Mark 6. Tie the meat neatly with kitchen twine. Heat the butter and oil in a roasting pan, add the meat, and cook, turning frequently, until browned all over. Season with salt and pepper, add the chopped celery, onion, carrot, and rosemary to the pan, and cook, stirring occasionally, for another 10 minutes. Pour in the wine and cook until it has evaporated. Cover, transfer to the oven, and roast for 30–40 minutes, depending on how well done you like your beef. After about 30 minutes the beef will be rare and after 40 minutes it will be medium.

Meanwhile, cook the chestnuts in boiling water until tender, then drain and press through a strainer (sieve) into a bowl.

Remove the meat from the roasting pan, let rest for 10 minutes, then remove the twine and carve into slices.

Place the roasting pan over low heat, stir in the cream and the chestnut purée, and cook, stirring frequently, until slightly thickened. Pour into a sauceboat and serve with the sliced meat.

Filetto al rosso trevigiano

Beef Tenderloin with Radicchio

Serves 4
Preparation: 15 minutes
Cooking: 25 minutes, plus
   5 minutes resting

olive oil, for oiling
1 lb 8½ oz/700 g beef tenderloin
   (fillet), cut in half lengthwise
12 oz/350 g radicchio from Treviso,
   cut into very thin strips,
   similar to matchsticks
7 oz/200 g Parmesan cheese,
   cut into thin slices
1 bunch parsley, chopped
juice of ½ lemon
salt and pepper

Photograph opposite

Preheat the oven to 350°F/180°C/Gas Mark 4 and oil a roasting pan with some olive oil.

Pound the beef with a meat tenderizer until you get 2 thin slices of the same size. Place one slice in the prepared roasting pan. Cover the meat with half the radicchio strips and half the Parmesan slices. Place the other slice on top and cover with the remaining radicchio strips and Parmesan slices. Season with salt and pepper, sprinkle with the chopped parsley, and cook in the oven for 25 minutes.

Remove from the oven and rest for 5 minutes. Remove the meat from the roasting pan, cut into slices, sprinkle with the lemon juice, and serve on a platter.

Arrosto alla crema di carciofi

Roasted Round of Beef with Artichoke Sauce

Serves 4
Preparation: 25 minutes
Cooking: 1 hour 45 minutes

5 tablespoons olive oil
2 tablespoons butter
1 sprig rosemary, chopped
2–3 sage leaves, chopped
1¾ lb/800 g beef eye of round
   (silverside)
½ cup (4 fl oz/120 ml) Cognac
1 cup (8 fl oz/250 ml) meat broth
   (stock), or as needed
8 artichoke hearts
1 onion, chopped
1 sprig parsley, chopped
salt and pepper

Preheat the oven to 350°F/180°C/Gas Mark 4. Heat 3 tablespoons of the oil and half the butter in a roasting pan over medium-high heat. Add the chopped rosemary and sage, then add the meat, and sear until browned all over. Season with salt and pepper. Pour in the Cognac and let it evaporate. Pour in a ladleful of hot broth (stock) and cook in the oven for 1 hour 20 minutes, adding more broth as needed to keep the sauce liquid.

Meanwhile, quarter the artichokes. Bring a pan of water to a boil, add the artichokes, and blanch for 5 minutes, then drain. Heat the remaining oil and butter in a skillet (frying pan) over medium heat, add the chopped onion and parsley, then add the drained artichokes and cook for 15 minutes. Remove from the heat and blend in a food processor or with a handheld blender until smooth.

Fifteen minutes before the cooking time is finished, pour the artichoke sauce into the roasting pan, frequently turning the meat. Cut the meat into thin slices, place in a serving dish, pour over the sauce, and serve.

Filetto al pesto prezzemolato

Beef Tenderloin with Parsley Pesto

Serves 6
Preparation: 20 minutes
Cooking: 20 minutes

1 lb 8½ oz/700 g beef tenderloin
  (fillet) in one single piece
olive oil, for brushing
salt and pepper

For the pesto:
2 bunches basil
1 bunch parsley
1 heaping tablespoon pine nuts
1 clove garlic, central core
  removed
olive oil, to taste
salt

Photograph opposite

Season the meat with salt and pepper, brush it with oil, and cook in a large skillet (frying pan) over medium heat for about 20 minutes, turning frequently, until cooked. Remove from the skillet and let rest.

Meanwhile, prepare the pesto by blending the basil, parsley, pine nuts, garlic, a pinch of salt and enough oil to achieve a dense sauce in a blender or food processor.

Cut the beef into slices, place in a serving dish, and cover with the pesto sauce. Serve.

Note: When using a whole clove of garlic, cut it in half and remove the central core. This makes the garlic easier to digest.

Filetto farcito ai funghi

Beef Tenderloin with Mushroom Stuffing

Serves 6
Preparation: 15 minutes, plus
  20 minutes soaking
Cooking: 30 minutes

2 oz/50 g dried porcini
2¼ lb/1 kg beef tenderloin (fillet)
2½ oz/70 g slices prosciutto
  crudo
2 oz/50 g Parmesan cheese,
  in shavings
1 sprig rosemary, leaves only,
  chopped
5 tablespoons olive oil
pat (knob) of butter
⅔ cup (5 fl oz/150 ml) white wine
salt

Soak the mushrooms in a bowl of lukewarm water for 20 minutes.

Preheat the oven to 350°F/180°C/Gas Mark 4. Using a sharp knife, cut a long slit three-quarters of the way through the beef, then open out like a book and pound with a meat tenderizer until the slice is thin, long, and tenderized.

Drain the mushrooms and pat dry with paper towels. Chop the mushrooms and sprinkle them over the pounded meat. Place the prosciutto slices on top, along with the Parmesan shavings and the chopped rosemary. Roll the slice up lengthwise, tie with kitchen twine, and season with salt.

Heat the oil and butter in a roasting pan over medium heat, add the meat, and once it has turned golden brown, splash with wine and let evaporate. Transfer to the oven and cook for 25 minutes. Serve.

Stracotto semplice

Pot-Roast Beef

Serves 4
Preparation: 15 minutes
Cooking: 1 hour 10 minutes

1 onion, cut into large chunks
1 carrot, cut into large chunks
2 stalks celery, cut into large
   chunks
1 ¾ lb/800 g chuck steak
4 tablespoons olive oil
½ cup (4 fl oz/120 ml) white wine,
   gently warmed
hot meat broth (stock), as needed
½ tablespoon all-purpose
   (plain) flour
pat (knob) of butter
salt and pepper

Put the vegetables and meat into a wide flameproof Dutch oven (casserole) with the oil and cook over high heat until golden. Add the gently warmed wine and let evaporate. Pour in enough hot broth (stock) to cover, then cover with a lid and cook for 1 hour. Season with salt and pepper and remove from the heat. Take the meat out of the Dutch oven and let rest.

Meanwhile, blend the cooking juices in a food processor or blender and pour into a clean pan. Mix the flour and butter together in a small bowl, add to the pan with the cooking juices, and heat over medium heat until it thickens.

Cut the meat into slices, place in a serving dish, and serve with the thickened cooking juices.

Note: If you would like to simplify the condiments, instead of mixing the flour with the butter, dissolve the flour in a ladleful of stock and add to the cooking juices.

Stracotto alla fiorentina

Florentine Beef Stew

Serves 6
Preparation: 30 minutes
Cooking: 2¼ hours

3 carrots
1 x 2¼-lb/1-kg lean beef, such
   as eye of round (topside)
1½ oz/40 g pancetta, cut
   into strips
1 stalk celery, chopped
½ onion, chopped
4 tablespoons olive oil
¾ cup (6 fl oz/175 ml) red wine
1 lb 2 oz/500 g (about 4) tomatoes,
   peeled, seeded, and chopped
salt and pepper

Photograph opposite

Cut a few long strips from one of the carrots and chop the remainder. Rub the piece of beef with salt and pepper. Place the carrot and pancetta strips on the meat and tie with kitchen twine.

Heat the oil in a large saucepan over medium heat. Add the chopped celery, onion, and carrots, then add the meat. Cook over high heat, turning the meat frequently, until browned all over. Pour in the wine and let evaporate. Add the tomatoes, reduce the heat, cover, and simmer gently for 2 hours.

Remove the meat from the pan, cut off the kitchen twine, carve, and place the slices in a warm serving dish. Pass the cooking juices and vegetables through a food mill and pour them over the meat.

Manzo alle Acciughe

Beef with Anchovies

Serves 6
Preparation: 30 minutes
Cooking: 3¼ hours

4 salted anchovies, washed
    and bones removed
grated nutmeg
juice of 1 lemon
2¼ lb/1 kg braising steak,
    such as chuck
2 tablespoons olive oil
⅔ cup (5 fl oz/150 ml) dry
    white wine

Chop 2 of the anchovies and season with some grated nutmeg and 3–4 drops of lemon juice. Using a sharp knife, make 10 cuts in the meat and insert the anchovy mixture. Heat the oil in a large flameproof pot, preferably made of earthenware, over low heat, add the remaining anchovies, and sprinkle with a little lemon juice. Cook, mixing with a fork until the anchovies dissolve. Add the meat and cook over medium-low heat for about 3 hours, splashing with wine occasionally and then several tablespoons of water. When the meat is cooked, remove the pot from the heat and serve immediately.

Note: You can make your own salt-cured anchovies. Use a quantity of salt that is equal to a quarter of the weight of the anchovies. Remove the head and entrails but leave the spine. Arrange the anchovies in clean, sterilized jars in dense layers, sprinkling each layer with salt. Seal with a lid and store in a cool place for at least 2 months, with a weight on the lid.

Spezzatino al vino e cipolle

Beef Stew with Wine and Onions

Serves 4
Preparation: 20 minutes
Cooking: 20 minutes

5 tablespoons (2½ oz/65 g) butter
6 onions, finely chopped
5 oz/150 g pancetta, diced
1 lb 5 oz/600 g lean stewing steak,
    such as chuck, cut into cubes
¼ cup (1 oz/25 g) all-purpose
    (plain) flour
scant 1⅔ cups (13 fl oz/375 ml)
    dry white wine
scant 1⅔ cups (13 fl oz/375 ml)
    red wine
salt and pepper

Melt the butter in a large pan, add the onions and pancetta, and cook over low heat, stirring occasionally, for 10 minutes. Stir in the meat, sprinkle with the flour, and cook, stirring continuously, for another 2 minutes. Gradually stir in the white and red wines and cook over low heat until the liquid is almost completely absorbed. Season with salt and pepper to taste and serve.

Girello alla crema di spinaci

Beef with Spinach Sauce

Serves 4
Preparation: 25 minutes
Cooking: 1½ hours

2 tablespoons olive oil
1 x 1¾ lb/800 g beef eye of
    round (topside) or another
    fairly lean cut
1⅔ cup (5 fl oz/150 ml) white wine
vegetable broth (stock), as needed
3 tablespoons butter
salt and pepper

For the sauce:
1¾ lb/800 g spinach, cooked
    and chopped
½ tablespoon all-purpose
    (plain) flour
scant ½ cup (3½ fl oz/100 ml) milk
⅓ cup (3 fl oz/80 ml) heavy
    (double) cream
2 egg yolks
⅓ cup (1 oz/30 g) freshly grated
    hard cheese, such as pecorino

Heat the oil in a saucepan with a lid over medium-low heat, add the meat, and sear until browned all over, turning it several times. Pour in the wine, let evaporate, and season with salt and pepper. Cover with the lid and cook for 1 hour, splashing with broth (stock) occasionally if the meat starts to dry out.

Meanwhile, preheat the oven to 350°F/180°C/Gas Mark 6. For the sauce, place the spinach in a saucepan, sprinkle with the flour, add the milk and cream, and season with salt. Gently simmer over low heat for about 15 minutes, or until all the liquid has been absorbed and the sauce has a creamy consistency. Pour the spinach mixture into a large bowl, add the egg yolks and grated cheese, and mix together to combine.

Remove the meat from the pan and cut into slices. Pour the meat cooking juices into a roasting pan, add the meat slices, cover with the spinach sauce, and cook in the oven for 15 minutes. Remove from the oven and serve in the roasting pan.

Stracotto di manzo alle pere

Braised Beef with Pears

Serves 4
Preparation: 15 minutes
Cooking: 40 minutes

1 tablespoon olive oil
1 onion, chopped
1¾ lb/800 g beef, sinews removed
    and cut into chunks
scant 1 cup (7 fl oz/200 ml) beer,
    such as stout
1 tablespoon red wine vinegar
½ tablespoon superfine (caster)
    sugar
aromatic herbs, such as thyme
    and bay leaves
2 pears, cut into small pieces
salt

Heat the oil in a pan over medium heat, add the onion, and sauté for 5 minutes, or until browned. Add the beef and cook over high heat for a few seconds, then pour in the beer. Add the vinegar and sugar, followed by the aromatic herbs. Reduce the heat to low, cover with a lid, and cook for 20 minutes, occasionally checking the quantity of liquid left. Add a little water if the pan starts to dry out. Add the pears to the pan and cook for another 10 minutes. Season with salt to taste and serve.

Polpette saporite alla birra

Meatballs Cooked in Beer

Serves 4
Preparation: 30 minutes
Cooking: 1 hour

7 oz/200 g stale bread, torn
    into chunks
full-fat (whole) milk, to soak
11 oz/300 g ground (minced) beef
11 oz/300 g sausage, removed
    from its casing and crumbled
2 eggs
few chives, chopped
1 sprig parsley, chopped
⅔ cup (3 oz/80 g) all-purpose
    (plain) flour
2 tablespoons olive oil
pat (knob) of butter
3 onions, chopped
4¼ cups (34 fl oz/1 liter) beer
1 tablespoon tomato paste (purée)
1 sprig thyme, leaves only
salt and pepper

Photograph opposite

Soak the bread in a little milk in a bowl for about 3 minutes, then drain. In another bowl, mix the ground (minced) beef with the crumbled sausage, eggs, drained bread, some of the chopped chives, and parsley. Season with salt and pepper.

Spread the flour out on a plate. Using damp hands, shape the mixture into balls, about the size of a walnut, and roll in the flour to coat. Heat the oil and butter in a large, deep skillet (frying pan) over medium heat, add the meatballs, and cook for about 10 minutes, or until golden brown. To brown the meatballs without them falling apart, shake repeatedly in the skillet so that they roll themselves in the oil and butter and brown on all sides. Do this in batches to avoid overcrowding the skillet. Remove from the skillet and set aside.

Add the chopped onions to the same skillet, pour in the beer, a little at a time, and let evaporate. Add the tomato paste (purée) and thyme leaves, and season with salt and pepper. Cook for 15 minutes then return the meatballs to the pan with the sauce, and cook for another 20 minutes. Sprinkle with chopped chives and serve.

Brasato alle cipolle

Braised Beef with Onions

Serves 6
Preparation: 30 minutes
Cooking: 2 hours

1 x 2¼-lb/1-kg beef eye of
    round (topside) or another
    fairly lean cut
1 oz/25 g pancetta, cut into
    thin strips
2¼ lb/1 kg onions, thickly sliced
salt and pepper
soft polenta (page 285),
    to serve (optional)

Using a knife, make several deep incisions in the beef and then insert the pancetta strips into the incisions and tie neatly with kitchen twine.

Put the onions in a large pan, place the meat on top, cover, and cook over very low heat for 1 hour. Turn the meat over, season well with salt and pepper, cover, and cook, stirring occasionally, for another 1 hour, or until tender.

Remove the meat from the pan, remove the kitchen twine, and carve into fairly thin slices. Place the slices, slightly overlapping, in a warm serving dish, spoon the onion sauce over them, and serve.

Note: If you prefer a more even consistency, pass the sauce through a food mill before serving.

Brasato al Barolo
Braised Beef with Barolo

Serves 6
Preparation: 15 minutes, plus
   6–7 hours marinating
Cooking: 1 hour 40 minutes

1 x 2¼-lb/1-kg beef eye of
   round (topside) or another
   fairly lean cut
3 tablespoons olive oil
3 tablespoons butter
3 tablespoons chopped
   prosciutto fat
pinch of unsweetened cocoa
   powder
1 teaspoon rum (optional)
salt

For the marinade:
1 bottle (3 cups/25 fl oz/750 ml)
   Barolo
2 carrots, sliced
2 onions, sliced
1 stalk celery, chopped
4 sage leaves
1 sprig small rosemary
1 bay leaf
10 black peppercorns
salt

Photograph opposite

Tie the meat neatly with kitchen twine, put into a large, deep dish, and pour in the wine for the marinade. Add the carrots, onions, celery, sage, rosemary, bay leaf, peppercorns, and a pinch of salt and let marinate for 6–7 hours. Drain the meat, reserving the marinade, and pat dry with paper towels.

Heat the oil, butter, and chopped prosciutto fat in a large flameproof Dutch oven (casserole), add the meat, and cook over high heat, turning frequently, until browned all over. Season with salt and pour in the reserved marinade. Reduce the heat, cover, and simmer for 1½ hours, or until tender.

Remove the meat from the Dutch oven, remove the kitchen twine, and carve. Arrange the slices, slightly overlapping, in a warm serving dish. Discard the herbs from the cooking liquid and pass through a food mill, then stir in the cocoa and rum, if using. Pour the sauce over the meat and serve.

Brasato

Braised Beef

Serves 6
Preparation: 4½ hours
Cooking: 2¼ hours

1 x 2¼-lb/1-kg beef eye of round
   (topside)
4 tablespoons butter
3 tablespoons olive oil
1 onion, finely chopped
2 carrots, finely chopped
1 celery stalk, finely chopped
¾ cup (175 ml/6 fl oz) red wine
1 ripe tomato, peeled and chopped
4 canned tomatoes, chopped
1 tablespoon tomato paste (purée)
4¼ cups (34 fl oz/1 liter) hot meat
   broth (stock)
salt and pepper

Tie the meat neatly with kitchen twine. Heat the butter and oil in a large flameproof Dutch oven (casserole), add the chopped onion, carrots, and celery, and cook over low heat, stirring occasionally, for 10 minutes. Add the meat and cook, turning frequently, until lightly browned. Season with salt and pepper, pour in the wine, and cook until it has evaporated, then add the fresh and canned tomatoes.

Mix the tomato paste (purée) with 5 tablespoons warm water in a bowl, add to the Dutch oven, and cook for an additional few minutes. Add enough stock to cover the meat halfway, bring to a boil, lower the heat, cover, and simmer for 1½ hours, adding more hot stock if the Dutch oven starts to dry out.

Remove the meat from the Dutch oven, remove the kitchen twine, and carve into slices. Place the slices in a warm serving dish, strain over the cooking juices, and serve.

Stinco al vino rosato

Beef Shank in Rosé

Serves 6
Preparation: 10 minutes
Cooking: 1 hour 10 minutes

1 x 2¼-lb/1-kg beef shank (shin)
all-purpose (plain) flour, for dusting
5 tablespoons olive oil
pat (knob) of butter
1 sprig rosemary
2 bay leaves
3 cloves garlic, unpeeled
8 black peppercorns
20 hazelnuts, dry-roasted, shelled,
   and crushed
2¼ cups (17 fl oz/500 ml) rosé wine
hot vegetable broth (stock),
   as needed
salt
Creamy Mashed Potatoes,
   (page 280), to serve

Photograph opposite

Dust the meat with flour, put into a colander, shake off any excess, and set aside.

Heat the oil and butter in a flameproof Dutch oven (casserole) over medium heat. Tie the rosemary and bay leaves together with kitchen twine and add to the Dutch oven. Add the garlic with its skin on, the peppercorns, and salt and cook for 5 minutes. Add the beef and cook until it is browned all over. Remove the garlic and add the crushed hazelnuts. Pour in the wine and let evaporate. Cover the Dutch oven with the lid and cook for about 1 hour, or until the meat starts falling off the bone. Add some hot broth (stock) occasionally, to prevent the Dutch oven from drying out.

Remove from the oven and let stand for 5 minutes. Place the meat on a platter, pour over the cooking juices, and serve with creamy mashed potatoes.

Veal

Veal is calf meat, usually from male dairy calves, although it can be of either sex. Because of its youth, the meat is very soft and tender, the animals not having used their muscles much. It's usually pale—from white to pink in color, due to its having largely been fed only milk, or not having eaten much solid food. Always buy humanely raised veal, and if you're not sure, ask the butcher if it's grass-fed or free-range.

Its leanness means it can benefit by having fat added to it in recipes—often pancetta in Italy, but unsmoked bacon works well too. Roasted Veal Tenderloin with Shallots (see page 94), for example, has smoked lard added to it. It's also often mixed with other, fattier meats in meat sauces and meatballs, particularly beef or pork. Cuts such as breast work well stuffed with other meats, variety meats (offal), and eggs, cheese, and spices.

Some Italian veal dishes are world famous, such as saltimbocca, where the veal is topped with prosciutto and a sage leaf and is served with capers and lemon. Milanese osso buco (see page 98) is another classic dish, made with cross-cut veal shanks (shins) braised with vegetables, white wine, and broth (stock), and topped with gremolata. It is sometimes served on risotto Milanese (saffron risotto).

Cuts

Veal is young and tender, and doesn't have the fat and marbling of beef, so it sometimes needs to be cooked a little differently. Shanks and shoulder of veal taste great when slow-cooked—both contain a lot of collagen in the tissue, which breaks down into a velvety sauce with falling apart meat. You can add to a stew or braise with vegetables and herbs, such as rosemary and sage. Short ribs also benefit from hours of slow-cooking—sear them first, then let them simmer. Veal chops are substantial, meaty and very versatile. Again, sear them first to seal in the moisture before roasting or broiling (grilling). Veal breast can be cooked on or off the bone. On requires slow-roasting; off and you should stuff it and tie with kitchen twine.

Italian cuts and cooking techniques

1 Codone o codoncino
Roasting

2 Sottofesa
Roasting, broiling (grilling), and sliced and roulades

3 Girello
Roasting, and sliced and scallops (escalopes)

4 Fesa francese
Broiling (grilling), and sliced, roulades, stuffed rolls, and scallops (escalopes)

5 Noce
Roasting, and chops, sliced, and scallops (escalopes)

6 Pesce o piccione
Boiling and stewing

7 Spinacino
Meat loaves and stuffed rolls and pockets

8 Nodini
Broiling (grilling)

9 Scamone
Roasting

10 Pancetta
Stuffed pockets

11 Punta di petto
Boiling and stewing

12 Geretto
Boiling, and chops with marrowbone

13 Fesa di spalla
Ideal sliced and for stuffed rolls

14 Costolette
Broiling (grilling), and chops and scallops (escalopes)

15 Fiocco
Stewing and braising

16 Reale
Roasting, boiling, stewing, and braising

17 Collo
Boiling and stewing

18 Fusello
Roasting, braising, boiling, and sliced

19 Cappello del prete
Boiling, stewing, and braising

20 Brione
Boiling, stewing, and braising

American cuts and cooking techniques

1 Blade
Braising, stewing, and ground (minced) meat

2 Shoulder
Roasting and diced for kabobs, pies, and meat loaf

3 Rib
Roasting and cut into chops for broiling (grilling) and frying

4 Loin
Roasting, and cut into chops or medallions for broiling (grilling) and frying

5 Sirloin
Roasting and cut into steaks

6 Rump roast
Roasting, and cut into round steaks and scallops (escalopes)

7 Leg
Roasting and pot roasting

8 Shank
Roasting and braising

9 Breast
Roasting, braising, stewing, and ground (minced) meat

10 Foreshank
Braising

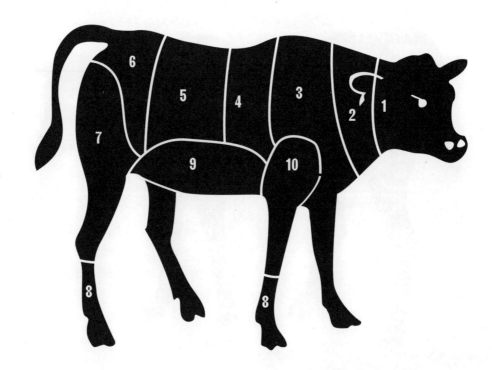

British cuts and cooking techniques

1 Head
Stewing

2 Scrag end
Casseroles and stocks, and chopped or ground (minced) for pies

3 Middle neck
Casseroles and stocks, and chopped or ground (minced) for pies

4 Best end
Roasting, and cut into cutlets (escalopes) for broiling (grilling) and frying

5 Loin
Roasting, and cut into chops and medallions for broiling (grilling) and frying

6 Rump
Roasting, and cut into steaks for broiling (grilling) and frying

7 Leg, silverside, topside
Roasting, pot-roasting, and cut into scallops (escalopes) and fillets for broiling (grilling) and frying

8 Knuckle, shin
Stewing, and chopped for pies

9 Breast
Roasting, braising, and stewing, and ground (minced)

10 Shoulder
Roasting

Arrosto di vitello

Roasted Veal

Serves 4
Preparation: 10 minutes
Cooking: 30 minutes, plus
  5 minutes resting

1 x 1¾ lb/800 g veal loin
1 tablespoon olive oil, plus
  extra for brushing
4 cloves garlic, unpeeled
6 basil leaves
½ tablespoon thyme leaves
salt and pepper

Preheat the oven to 425°F/220°C/Gas Mark 7. Heat a large skillet (frying pan) over high heat, brush the meat with oil, and brown it all over before placing it in a roasting pan with the oil. Add the garlic, basil, thyme, and salt and pepper, and cover with foil. Place the pan in the oven and cook for 25 minutes, basting the meat twice with its cooking juices. Remove the meat from the oven, let rest for 5 minutes, then carve it into slices. Place the slices in a serving dish and pour over the cooking juices.

Note: Depending on personal preference, serve the veal with the caramelized garlic cloves.

Arrosto di vitello al parmigiano

Roasted Veal with Parmesan Cheese

Serves 6
Preparation: 25 minutes
Cooking: 1 hour 40 minutes,
  plus 20 minutes resting

1¾ lb/800 g veal rump roast
  (silverside)
2½ oz/70 g Parmesan cheese,
  cut into matchsticks
2 tablespoons olive oil
5 oz/150 g veal scallop (escalope)
2 stalks celery, chopped
1 cup (8 fl oz/250 ml) dry
  white wine
vegetable broth (stock), as needed
scant ½ cup (3½ fl oz/100 ml)
  light (single) cream
salt and pepper
sage leaves, to garnish

Photograph opposite

Make several incisions in the veal rump roast and insert a stick of cheese into each one along with a pinch of pepper.

Heat the oil in a nonstick skillet (frying pan) over high heat, add the veal rump roast, and sear on all sides. Transfer to an oval-shape flameproof Dutch oven (casserole) and add the slices of veal scallop (escalope) and the chopped celery.

Heat the wine in a saucepan until warm, then pour it into the Dutch oven and let evaporate over high heat. Pour in enough broth (stock) until it just covers the meat, bring to a simmer, then cover with a lid and cook over medium heat for 15 minutes. Season with salt and pepper, reduce the heat to medium-low, and cook for another 1¼ hours. Remove the meat from the Dutch oven, wrap it in foil, and rest for 20 minutes.

Meanwhile, blend the cooking juices in a food processor or with a handheld blender. Pour the mixture into a saucepan, add the cream, and simmer until the sauce is reduced to a smooth creamy consistency.

To serve, carve the meat into slices and place them in a serving dish. Add a good spoonful of the sauce between each slice and garnish with sage leaves.

Arrosto al funghi
Roasted Veal with Mushrooms

Serves 4
Preparation: 25 minutes
Cooking: 1 hour 20 minutes

1¾ lb/800 g veal chuck steak
pinch of grated nutmeg
3 tablespoons butter
3 cloves garlic, chopped
½ cup (4 fl oz/120 ml) brandy
scant 1 cup (7 fl oz/200 ml)
    vegetable broth (stock)
1 lb 5 oz/600 g porcini, cleaned,
    patted dry, and cut into slices
    ¼ inch/5 mm thick
3 sprigs marjoram, chopped
1 bunch parsley, chopped
salt and pepper
Sautéed Jerusalem artichokes
    (page 264), to serve

Preheat the oven to 350°F/180°C/Gas Mark 4. Season the veal with a pinch of salt, pepper, and grated nutmeg. Melt the butter in a large flameproof Dutch oven (casserole) and once foaming, add the meat and garlic and cook until the meat is browned all over. Add the brandy and simmer until it has evaporated. Pour in the broth (stock), then cook in the oven for 30 minutes. Add the mushrooms with a pinch of salt and cook for another 20 minutes.

Arrange the meat and two-thirds of the mushrooms in a warm serving dish. Using a handheld blender, blend the cooking juices and the remaining mushrooms, then add the chopped marjoram and parsley and stir. Cut the meat into slices and cover with the sauce. Serve with the Jerusalem artichokes.

Carré ai funghi
Veal Loin with Mushrooms

Serves 6
Preparation: 15 minutes
Cooking: 1½ hours

1 x 3-lb/1.3-kg veal loin
    with 4 cutlets
2 cloves garlic, halved
2 tablespoons olive oil
1 sprig rosemary
1 sprig sage
2 tablespoons butter
⅔ cup (5 fl oz/150 ml) white wine
11 oz/300 g porcini
5 potatoes, diced
7 oz/200 g pumpkin, peeled,
    seeded, and diced
salt and pepper

Photograph opposite

Preheat the oven 400°F/200°F/Gas Mark 6. Using a sharp knife, make 4 incisions in the meat and insert the halved garlic cloves. Season with salt and pepper.

Pour the oil into a roasting pan, add the rosemary and sage sprigs, and place the meat on top. Add small curls of butter, splash with the wine, and cook in the oven for 1½ hours, basting the meat with warm water, if the pan starts to dry out.

Thirty minutes before the end of the cooking time, remove the sage and rosemary sprigs, add the mushrooms, diced potatoes, and pumpkin to the pan, and return to the oven. When done, remove the roasting pan from the oven, place the meat in a serving dish with the vegetables, and serve.

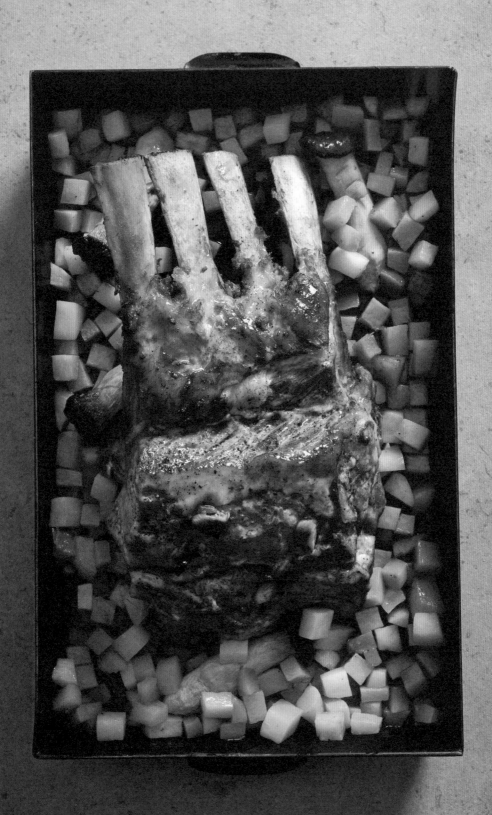

Arrosto in salsa d'oro

Roasted Veal with Egg Yolk Sauce

Serves 4–6
Preparation: 25 minutes
Cooking: 1 hour 20 minutes

2¼ lb/1 kg veal sirloin (rump)
2 oz/50 g prosciutto crudo, in
    one slice, cut into matchsticks
1 sprig rosemary
1 sprig parsley
zest of 1 lemon
4 tablespoons olive oil
2¼ cups (17 fl oz/500 ml) cold
    vegetable broth (stock)
2 egg yolks
salt and pepper

Using a sharp knife, make several incisions in the meat and insert the prosciutto into each one. Season with salt and pepper and tie with kitchen twine.

Finely chop the rosemary, parsley, and lemon zest and put into a heavy saucepan with the oil. Cook over medium heat until the herbs color. Pour in ½ cup (4 fl oz/120 ml) of the cold vegetable broth (stock) and bring to a boil over high heat. Add the meat, reduce the heat to low, and cook for 1¼ hours. Remove from the heat, set the meat aside, and keep warm.

Too make the sauce, let the cooking juices cool, then blend with a handheld blender. Add 1 egg yolk at a time to the blended juices, stirring to prevent lumps from forming. After adding the egg yolks to the cold cooking liquid, warm over low heat while stirring continuously until the sauce starts to thicken. Do not let it boil at any stage.

Cut the meat into slices, place in a serving dish, and pour over the egg yolk sauce.

Note: When zesting a lemon, be careful to use only the yellow part because the white pith is bitter.

Arrosto in crosta di pasta di pane
Veal in a Bread Crust

Serves 6
Preparation: 35 minutes, plus
  20 minutes soaking
Cooking time: 2 hours 10 minutes

1 x 2¼ lb/1 kg veal shoulder
4 tablespoons butter
3 cloves garlic
1 sprig rosemary
2 sage leaves
½ cup (4 fl oz/120 ml) white wine
½ cup (4 fl oz/120 ml) brandy
1 egg, separated
salt and pepper

For the bread dough:
11 oz/300 g strong white flour
1 teaspoon salt
¼ oz/10 g active dry (fast-action
  dried) yeast
1 tablespoon olive oil, plus extra
  for oiling

For the stuffing:
2 oz/50 g dried mushrooms
pat (knob) of butter
vegetable broth (stock), as
  needed (optional)
1 cup (7 oz/200 g) white rice
3–4 tablespoons grated Parmesan
  cheese

Tie the meat with kitchen twine and set aside. Melt the butter in a large flameproof Dutch oven (casserole) over medium heat, add the garlic cloves, rosemary, and sage, and gently fry briefly. Place the meat in the Dutch oven and cook until browned all over. Pour in the wine, let it evaporate, and cook for 20 minutes, turning occasionally. Baste the meat with the brandy and cook for another 40 minutes, turning it regularly and adding a little hot water if the pan starts to dry out. Remove the meat from the heat and let cool to room temperature. When the roast is cold, cut into thick slices.

To make the bread dough, mix the flour, salt, and yeast in a large bowl. Make a well in the centre, then add the oil and ⅔ cup (5 fl oz/ 150 ml) water, and mix well. Knead for about 10 minutes, or until a smooth and elastic dough forms. It should not be too soft. Shape the dough into a ball and leave to rise in a clean oiled bowl, covered with a damp dish towel, for 30 minutes at room temperature.

Meanwhile, prepare the stuffing. Soak the dried mushrooms in a small bowl of lukewarm water for 20 minutes. Drain, set the water aside, and pat the mushrooms dry. In a small skillet (frying pan) sauté the mushrooms in the butter for 5 minutes. Add a few spoonfuls of the veal pan juices or some stock (broth) and cook for 5 minutes. Remove the mushrooms from the pan and finely chop.

Strain the reserved mushroom water into a saucepan, put over high heat (adding some more hot water if needed), and bring to a boil. Add the rice and cook for 10–12 minutes, or according to package directions, until tender, then transfer to a food processer and blend. Add the chopped mushrooms and grated cheese to the blended rice and season with salt and pepper, to taste.

Preheat the oven to 400°F/200°F/Gas Mark 6.

Roll out the bread dough on a baking sheet to a thickness of ⅛ inch/3–4 mm. Lay a sheet of kitchen foil on top of the dough and place the roasted meat slices onto the foil, alternating with about a handful of the rice stuffing until all are used up. Wrap everything in the foil and then in the bread dough. Seal the dough with the egg white and brush with the yolk. Cook in the oven for 35 minutes. Remove from the oven, cut open the dough and remove the foil-wrapped meat and stuffing. Arrange the meat and stuffing on a serving dish, drizzle with any remaining juices, and serve.

Note: If you are in Italy, you can simply buy 1 lb 2 oz/500 g bread dough readymade because it is often sold fresh in grocery stores.

Girello in salsa Chardonnay

Veal in Chardonnay Sauce

Serves 6
Preparation: 20 minutes
Cooking: 1 hour

1 lb 10 oz/750 g veal eye of
    round steak (silverside)
1½ tablespoons butter
1 stalk celery, diced
2 carrots, diced
2 zucchini (courgettes), diced
salt and pepper

For the sauce:
1½ tablespoons butter
2 shallots, chopped
1 bottle (3 cups/25 fl oz/750 ml)
    Chardonnay
juice of 1 lemon
1¼ tablespoons cornstarch
    (cornflour)
Tabasco sauce, to taste
1⅓ cups (11 oz/300 g) mayonnaise

Photograph opposite

Preheat the oven to 300°F/150°C/Gas Mark 2. Melt the butter in a small flameproof Dutch oven (casserole) over medium heat. Remove from the heat and brush the melted butter over the meat. Wrap the meat in kitchen foil, place on a baking sheet, and cook in the oven for 40 minutes. Remove the meat from the oven and let rest inside the kitchen foil.

Meanwhile, bring a pan of salted water to a boil, add the diced vegetables, and blanch for 2 minutes, then drain and set aside.

For the sauce, heat the butter in a pan over low heat, add the chopped shallots, and cook for 10 minutes, or until they have turned soft and translucent. Pour in the wine and lemon juice and cook until the liquid is reduced by half.

Mix the cornstarch (cornflour) with 2 tablespoons lukewarm water in a bowl, then add to the pan. Season with salt and pepper, and add several drops of Tabasco, to taste. Mix and strain the sauce into a clean pan. Return to low heat and when lukewarm, mix in the mayonnaise.

Cut the meat into slices and place in a serving dish. Cover with the sauce and grind over some black pepper. Serve with the blanched vegetables arranged around the meat.

Filetto in crosta di prosciutto e fave

Veal Tenderloin Wrapped in Prosciutto and Fava Beans

Serves 4
Preparation: 20 minutes
Cooking: 50 minutes, plus
**   10 minutes resting**

11 oz/300 g fava (broad) beans,
    shelled (about 1 cup)
2 shallots, cut into slices
6–8 tablespoons extra virgin
    olive oil
1 lb 8½ oz/700 g veal tenderloin
    (fillet)
3½ oz/100 g prosciutto crudo,
    in slices
⅔ cup (5 fl oz/150 ml) white wine
salt and pepper
Sautéed Puntarelle (page 256),
    to serve

Photograph opposite

Preheat the oven to 350°F/180°F/Gas Mark 4 and line a roasting pan with parchment paper.

Bring a pan of water to a boil, add the fava (broad) beans, and blanch for 5 minutes, then drain and let cool. Pop the beans out of their thick skins into a bowl and discard the skins.

Gently cook the sliced shallots in a pan with 2–3 tablespoons oil and 4–5 tablespoons water. Add the fava beans and season with salt. Cook for 5–6 minutes, then remove from the heat and blend with a handheld blender until a smooth creamy consistency is achieved. Let cool.

Season the veal, then cover evenly with the fava bean sauce. Lay the prosciutto slices on a sheet of parchment paper, overlapping slightly. Place the veal on top and wrap in the prosciutto with the help of the paper. Tie the meat securely with kitchen twine and transfer to the prepared roasting pan. Add the remaining oil and the white wine and cook in the oven for 35 minutes.

Remove the meat from the oven, then let rest for 10 minutes. Carve the meat into slices, place in a serving dish, and serve with the cooking juices and the sautéed puntarelle.

Filetto di vitello al forno con scalogni

Roasted Veal Tenderloin with Shallots

Serves 4
Preparation: 15 minutes
Cooking: 45 minutes

8 small shallots
2 tablespoons olive oil
1¾ lb/800 g veal tenderloin (fillet)
2 slices smoked lard, chopped
1 sprig parsley
1 bunch sage and thyme
salt

Preheat the oven to 425°F/220°C/Gas Mark 7. Bring a pan of lightly salted water to a boil and add the shallots. Blanch for 3 minutes, then drain and set aside.

Heat the oil in a flameproof Dutch oven (casserole) over high heat, add the veal, and sear the meat until it is golden all over. Add the chopped lard, the drained shallots, and the herbs, then cover the Dutch oven with kitchen foil and secure firmly with kitchen twine. Cook in the oven for 35 minutes.

Remove from the oven, remove the foil and twine, and place the veal on a cutting (chopping) board. Carve the meat into thin slices and place in a serving dish with the shallots around the meat.

Note: The cooking time can be halved by cooking the shallots and the veal in a pressure cooker for 10–13 minutes from when it first starts to whistle.

Stinco arrosto

Roasted Shank of Veal

Serves 6
Preparation: 15 minutes
Cooking: 2 hours 20 minutes

3 tablespoons olive oil
3 tablespoons butter
1 sprig myrtle or 6 juniper berries
1 sprig rosemary
2 shallots, finely chopped
1 veal shank (shin)
¾ cup (6 fl oz/175 ml) red wine
salt and pepper

Preheat the oven to 375°F/190°C/Gas Mark 5. Put the oil, butter, myrtle or juniper berries, rosemary, and shallots into a roasting pan and cook over low heat, stirring occasionally, for 10 minutes. Add the veal and cook, turning frequently, until golden brown on all sides. Season with salt and pepper, transfer to the oven, and roast for 1 hour. Pour in the wine, return the pan to the oven, and roast, basting occasionally, for another 1 hour. If necessary, add a ladleful of hot water.

Remove the veal from the oven and carve it, then place the slices in a warm serving dish and spoon the cooking juices over them.

Arrosto di codino tonnato

Roasted Veal with Tuna Sauce

Serves 6
Preparation: 30 minutes
Cooking: 1½ hours

3 tablespoons olive oil
2¼ lb/1 kg veal tail
1 bunch scallions (spring onions)
⅔ cup (5 fl oz/150 ml) dry
    white wine
lukewarm meat broth (stock),
    as needed
5 oz/150 g tuna in oil, drained
1 salted anchovy, washed
    and boned
juice of 1 lemon
salt and pepper

Preheat the oven to 400°F/200°F/Gas Mark 6. Put the oil into a roasting pan. Place the veal tail in the pan, add the scallions (spring onions), and season with salt and pepper. Put into the oven and, when the meat has browned, reduce the oven temperature to 350°F/180°C/Gas Mark 4, pour in the wine and continue cooking. If the pan starts to dry out, pour in a little lukewarm broth (stock). After 30 minutes, add the tuna and anchovy to the roasting pan, and cook for another 30 minutes.

Remove the roasting pan from the oven and cut the meat into slices. Blend the tuna, anchovy, and cooking juices with a handheld blender, add the lemon juice, and pour over the sliced meat. Serve.

Note: Less prized chunks of tuna known in Italian as *buzzonaglia* can also be used for the sauce. Obtained from tuna scraps in oil, these tuna chunks are much more flavorsome than tuna fillet.

Spezzatino di vitello

Veal Stew

Serves 6
Preparation: 20 minutes
Cooking: 1¼ hours

1¾ lb/800 g veal stew meat
    (stewing steak)
all-purpose (plain) flour, for dusting
4 tablespoons extra virgin olive oil
1 bay leaf
½ cup (4 fl oz/120 ml) red wine
1 carrot, finely chopped
1 onion, finely chopped
1 stalk celery, finely chopped
⅓ cup (2 oz/50 g) tomato paste
    (purée)
1¼ cups (10 fl oz/300 ml) vegetable
    broth (stock), optional
salt and pepper
Polenta (page 285), boiled rice,
    couscous, or Creamy Mashed
    Potato (page 280), to serve

Dust the meat with flour, put into a colander, and shake off any excess. Heat the oil in a deep skillet (frying pan) over medium heat, add the meat, sear until it is brown all over. Do this in batches if there is not enough space in your pan to brown all pieces at once. Return the meat to the pan, add the bay leaf, pour in the red wine, and cook until the wine has almost evaporated. Add the chopped vegetables, then season with salt and pepper. Add the tomato paste (purée) and mix it with the cooking juices. Reduce the heat to low, cover with a lid, and cook for 1 hour, checking regularly and adding hot water if the stew starts to dry out.

Transfer the stew to a serving dish and serve with polenta, boiled rice, mashed potato, or couscous.

Note: If the juices reduce too much during cooking, slowly add some boiling water to the stew until you get the right consistency. Season to taste.

Spezzatino con olive e cipolline

Veal Stew with Olives and Onions

Serves 4
Preparation: 10 minutes
Cooking: 50 minutes

2 tablespoons olive oil
1¾ lb/800 g veal, diced
24 pearl (baby) onions
1½ cups (5 oz/150 g) pitted
   green olives, sliced
salt and pepper

Photograph opposite

Heat the oil in a large flameproof Dutch oven (casserole) over medium heat, add the meat, increase the heat to high, and cook for 5 minutes, stirring, or until browned all over. Cover, reduce the heat to low, and cook for 25 minutes. Add the pearl (baby) onions and sliced olives, season with salt and pepper, and cook, covered, for another 20 minutes. Serve.

Note: The easiest way to peel pearl (baby) onions is to blanch them in a pan of boiling water for a few minutes, drain, and let cool slightly before peeling.

Spezzatino con piselli

Veal Stew with Peas

Serves 4
Preparation: 30 minutes
Cooking: 55 minutes

1 lb/8½ oz/700 g veal stew meat
   (stewing steak)
all-purpose (plain) flour, for dusting
2 tablespoons butter
½ cup (4 fl oz/120 ml) white wine
1 white onion, thinly sliced
3 cups (14 oz/400 g) shelled peas
1¼ cups (10 fl oz/300 ml) hot
   vegetable broth (stock)
salt

Dust the meat with the flour, put into a colander, and shake off any excess. Heat the butter in a flameproof Dutch oven (casserole) over high heat until foaming, then add the meat and cook until it is browned all over. Season with salt to taste, pour in the white wine, and let evaporate gently. Add the onion and peas, then pour in scant 1 cup (7 fl oz/200 ml) of the hot vegetable broth (stock). Reduce the heat to low, cover with the lid, and cook for 45 minutes, adding more hot broth (stock) if needed.

Note: Make sure the broth (stock) is very hot when it is added to the meat so it doesn't slow down the cooking process. If you want, you can substitute the white onion with 2–3 scallions (spring onions), thinly sliced.

Ossibuchi alla Milanese

Milanese Osso Buco

Serves 4
Preparation: 20 minutes
Cooking: 1 hour

4 osso buco (2-inch/5-cm-thick
    rounds of veal shank/knuckle)
all-purpose (plain) flour, for dusting
6 tablespoons butter
½ onion, chopped
5 tablespoons dry white wine
¾ cup (6 fl oz/175 ml) meat broth
    (stock)
1 stalk celery, chopped
1 carrot, chopped
2 tablespoons tomato paste
    (purée)
salt and pepper

For the gremolata:
thinly peeled zest of ½ lemon,
    finely chopped
1 sprig flat-leaf parsley, finely
    chopped

Photograph opposite

Dust the veal shanks with flour, put into a colander, and shake off any excess. Set aside.

Melt the butter in a large pan, add the chopped onion, and cook over low heat for 5 minutes, stirring occasionally. Add the veal to the pan and cook over high heat, turning frequently, until browned all over. Season with salt and pepper and cook for another few minutes, then pour in the wine and cook until it has evaporated. Pour in the broth (stock) and add the chopped celery and carrot. Reduce the heat, cover, and simmer for 30 minutes, adding more broth, if the pan starts to dry out.

Mix the tomato paste (purée) with 1 tablespoon hot water in a small bowl and stir into the pan.

Prepare the gremolata by combining the lemon zest and parsley in a small bowl. Add the mixture to the veal, turn carefully, and cook for another 5 minutes. Serve.

Spezzatino con verdure

Veal and Vegetable Stew

Serves 4
Preparation: 20 minutes
Cooking: 1¼ hours

2 tablespoons olive oil
2 tablespoons butter
1 onion, finely chopped
1 stalk celery, finely chopped
1 lb 5 oz/600 g boned veal shoulder,
    cut into cubes
all-purpose (plain) flour, for dusting
3 carrots, cut into thin sticks
scant ½ cup (3½ fl oz/100 ml)
    puréed canned tomatoes
    (passata)
3 zucchini (courgettes), cut into
    thin sticks
salt and pepper

Photograph opposite

Heat the oil and butter in a large saucepan, add the onion and celery, and cook over low heat for 5 minutes, stirring occasionally.

Dust the veal with flour, put into a colander, and shake off any excess. Add to the pan and cook over high heat, stirring frequently, until browned all over. Season with salt and pepper and cook for another few minutes, then add the carrots and tomatoes. Reduce the heat, cover, and simmer for 45 minutes, occasionally adding 2–3 tablespoons warm water if the stew starts to dry out. Add the zucchini (courgettes), cover, and cook for another 15 minutes. Serve.

Spezzatino ai sei profumi

Six-Aroma Veal Stew

Serves 4
Preparation: 30 minutes, plus
    2 hours marinating
Cooking: 50 minutes

1¾ lb/800 g boneless veal shoulder,
    cut into cubes
1 clove garlic, chopped
1 sprig flat-leaf parsley, chopped
1 sprig basil, chopped
juice of 1 lemon, strained
juice of 1 orange, strained
grated zest of 1 lime
1 tablespoon cumin seeds
3 tablespoons olive oil
3 tablespoons butter
salt and pepper

Season the veal with salt and pepper and put into a large bowl with the chopped garlic, parsley, and basil. Add the lemon and orange juice, lime zest, and cumin seeds and mix well. Let the veal marinate for 2 hours, stirring occasionally.

Heat the oil and butter in a large pan. Drain the veal and reserve the marinade. Add the meat to the pan, and cook, stirring frequently, for 5 minutes, or until browned on all sides. Strain the reserved marinade into the pan, cover, and simmer for 45 minutes, adding a little warm water if the stew starts to dry out. Serve.

Polpettine vellutate allo zafferano

Meatballs in a Saffron Cream

Serves 6
Preparation: 20 minutes
Cooking: 30 minutes

1 lb 5 oz/600 g ground
   (minced) veal
1 sprig parsley, chopped
1 egg
all-purpose (plain) flour,
   for coating
2 tablespoons olive oil
1 onion, chopped
½ cup (4 fl oz/120 ml) dry
   white wine
⅓ cup (2½ fl oz/70 ml) heavy
   (double) cream
few saffron threads
salt and pepper
mixed salad greens (leaves),
   to serve

Photograph opposite

Combine the ground (minced) veal with the chopped parsley and the egg in a large bowl, and season with salt and pepper.

Spread the flour out on a large plate. Using damp hands, shape the meat mixture into balls the size of a walnut and roll in the flour to coat. Heat the oil in a saucepan over medium heat, add the chopped onion and the meatballs, and turn them gently. Cook for about 10 minutes, or until the meatballs are golden brown, then add the wine and let evaporate. Add ½ cup (4 fl oz/120 ml) lukewarm water and cook for another 15 minutes.

Pour the cream into a bowl. In another bowl, place the saffron and 1 tablespoon lukewarm water and stir together. Add to the cream, stir, and pour everything into the saucepan with the meatballs. Cook for another 5 minutes, then serve with a side salad.

Arrosto al latte e prosciutto

Veal Braised in Milk with Prosciutto

Serves 6
Preparation: 15 minutes
Cooking: 1¼ hours

3 tablespoons butter
2 tablespoons all-purpose (plain)
   flour
2 slices prosciutto, cut into thin
   strips
1 x 1¾-lb/800-g boneless veal
   breast
3¾ cups (30 fl oz/900 ml) milk
salt
mixed salad greens (leaves),
   to serve (optional)

Photograph opposite

Melt the butter in a large pan, stir in the flour, then add the prosciutto and cook, stirring continuously, until browned. Tie the veal with kitchen twine, add to the pan, and cook over high heat, turning frequently, until browned all over. Season with salt to taste.

Pour in ¾ cup (6 fl oz/175 ml) of the milk and cook until it has been absorbed. Repeat this three times without covering the pan, each time waiting until the milk has all been absorbed. Finally, add the remaining milk and cook until it has almost all been absorbed.

Remove the veal from the pan and remove the kitchen twine. Carve the meat into slices and serve with the cooking juices and mixed salad greens (leaves).

Spinacino ripieno

Stuffed Veal Breast

Serves 4
Preparation: 30 minutes
Cooking: 45 minutes

3½ cups (3½ oz/100 g) spinach
scant 1 cup (7 oz/200 g) sheep
   ricotta
1 egg
3½ oz/100 g smoked cooked ham,
   chopped
1 oz/30 g pecorino cheese, grated
1 x 1 lb 5 oz/600 g veal breast
3 tablespoons butter
½ cup (4 fl oz/120 ml) white port
8 shallots, peeled and cut in half
scant 1 cup (7 fl oz/200 ml)
   vegetable broth (stock)
salt and pepper
Asparagus and Sweet Mustard
   (page 264), to serve

Preheat the oven to 350°F/180°C/Gas Mark 4. Bring a pan of salted water to a boil, add the spinach, and blanch for 2 minutes. Drain and let cool. Pat the spinach dry and chop finely. Mix the spinach with the ricotta in a large bowl. Add a pinch of salt, some pepper, the egg, the chopped ham, and the pecorino cheese, and mix all the ingredients together. Fill a pastry (piping) bag with the mixture and stuff the meat. Sew the open side closed with a trussing needle and thick white thread.

Melt the butter in a flameproof Dutch oven (casserole) over medium heat, add the meat, and sear for 10 minutes, or until browned on all sides. Pour the port over the meat and add the halved shallots. Pour in the broth (stock), season with salt and pepper, and cook in the oven for 35 minutes. Remove the meat from the oven, let cool, then serve with asparagus and sweet mustard.

Note: This cut of veal breast near the tail forms a natural "pocket" that should be kept intact for this recipe.

Arrosto alle olive
Braised Veal with Olives

Serves 6
Preparation: 35 minutes
Cooking: 1 hour 25 minutes,
   plus 10 minutes resting

1 x 1¾-lb/800-g veal round
   (topside)
2 cups (7 oz/200 g) pitted
   and halved green olives
2 tablespoons olive oil
4 tablespoons butter
1 onion, chopped
1 carrot, chopped
1 stalk celery, chopped
1 sprig rosemary, chopped
¾ cup (6 fl oz/175 ml) dry
   white wine
salt and pepper
hot broth (stock), to thin (optional)
1–2 tablespoons butter (optional)
1–2 tablespoons all-purpose (plain)
   flour (optional)

Photograph opposite

Make small incisions in the veal with a small, sharp knife, insert the olive halves, and tie neatly with kitchen twine.

Heat the oil and butter in a large pan, add the chopped onion, carrot, celery, and rosemary, and cook over low heat, stirring occasionally, for 10 minutes. Add the meat and cook, turning frequently, until browned all over. Pour in the wine and cook until it has evaporated, then season with salt and pepper. Simmer gently over low heat for 1 hour, turning occasionally and adding a little warm water if the stew starts to dry out.

Remove the veal from the pan and let rest for 10 minutes. Remove the kitchen twine, carve the meat into slices, and place in a warm serving dish.

Pass the cooking juices through a food mill into a bowl. If they are too thick, thin with a little hot broth (stock); if they are too runny, add a paste of equal quantities of butter and all-purpose (plain) flour. Spoon the juices over the meat and serve.

Arrosto di girello
Braised Veal Round

Serves 6
Preparation: 30 minutes
Cooking: 1 hours 40 minutes,
   plus 10 minutes resting

1 x 1¾-lb/800 g veal
   round (topside)
4 tablespoons butter
1 oz/25 g pancetta, sliced
1 onion, thinly sliced
3 carrots, thinly sliced
1 bunch herbs, chopped
¾ cup (6 fl oz/175 ml) dry
   white wine
salt and pepper

Tie the veal with kitchen twine. Melt the butter in a large pan, add the veal, and cook, turning frequently, for about 10 minutes, or until browned all over. Season with salt and pepper and remove the veal from the pan.

Place the pancetta on the bottom of the pan, return the veal to the pan, cover with the onion and carrots, and add the herbs. Pour in ¾ cup (6 fl oz/175 ml) warm water and the wine, cover, and simmer over low heat for about 1½ hours.

Remove the veal and let rest for about 10 minutes. Pour the cooking juices into a food processor and process to a purée. Remove the kitchen twine, carve the veal into slices, and place in a warm serving dish. Spoon the purée over the veal and serve.

Stinco al sidro

Veal Shank in Cider

Serves 6
Preparation: 10 minutes
Cooking: 2 hours

1¼ sticks (5 oz/150 g) butter
4 shallots, thinly sliced
1 veal shank
1 tablespoon Calvados or applejack
4¼ cups (34 fl oz/1 litre) hard
   (dry) cider
11 oz/300 g pearl (baby) onions
4 red apples, cored and diced
1 cup (8 fl oz/250 ml) heavy
   (double) cream
1 egg yolk
salt and pepper
herbs of your choice, to garnish

Photograph opposite

Melt 4 tablespoons (2 oz/50 g) of the butter in a large pan, add
the shallots, and cook over low heat, stirring occasionally, for
10 minutes. Increase the heat to high, add the veal shank (shin),
and cook, turning frequently, for 10 minutes, until browned all over.
Season with salt and pepper, add the Calvados or applejack, and
cook until it has evaporated. Pour in the hard (dry) cider, add a little
more salt, reduce the heat, cover, and simmer for 1½ hours.

Meanwhile, melt 4 tablespoons (2 oz/50 g) of the remaining butter
in another pan, add the onions, and cook over low heat, stirring
occasionally, for 15 minutes. Melt the remaining butter in a third
pan, add the diced apples, and cook over low heat, stirring
occasionally, until just tender.

Remove the meat from the pan and keep warm. Stir the cream
into the cooking juices, then stir in the egg yolk and heat gently
without letting the sauce boil. Carve the veal, place the slices in
a warm serving dish, pour the sauce over them, and surround with
the apples and onions. Garnish with herbs of your choice and serve.

Filetto in casseruola

Veal Casserole

Serves 4
Preparation: 20 minutes
Cooking: 30 minutes, plus
   5 minutes resting

2¼ lb/1 kg veal tenderloin (fillet)
2 tablespoons olive oil
2 tablespoons butter, plus
   a pat (knob)
1 sprig rosemary
2 bay leaves
½ lemon
2½ tablespoons all-purpose
   (plain) flour
½ cup (4 fl oz/120 ml) dry white
   wine or 2 tablespoons white
   wine vinegar
salt and pepper

Season the veal with salt and pepper. Put it into a flameproof Dutch
oven (casserole) with the oil, 2 tablespoons butter, the rosemary,
bay leaves, and lemon. Cover and cook over high heat for 25 minutes,
turning the meat occasionally. Uncover and remove the lemon,
rosemary, and bay leaves. Mix the pat (knob) of butter and the flour
together in a small bowl, then stir it into the Dutch oven. Pour the
wine or vinegar over the meat and let evaporate. Cook over high heat
for 5 minutes to reduce the sauce.

Remove from the heat and rest the meat for 5 minutes, then cut into
slices (not too thin), place in a serving dish, and serve with its juices.

Note: Tie the rosemary and bay leaves together with several rounds
of kitchen twine so that the rosemary doesn't lose its leaves during
cooking and the herbs can be easily removed.

Entrecôte con pancetta al profumo d'arancia

Orange-Scented Entrecôte with Pancetta

Serves 4
Preparation: 15 minutes
Cooking: 30 minutes

6 anchovies fillets in oil
2 unwaxed oranges
1 bunch parsley, leaves only and
    finely chopped
4 x 5-oz/150-g slices veal rump
    slices
3½ oz/100 g slices pancetta
2 sprigs rosemary, leaves chopped
salt and pepper

For the mixed salad with herbs:
5 cups (5 oz/150 g) mixed salad
    greens (leaves) with herbs, such
    as mint, wild fennel, and basil
1 tablespoon balsamic vinegar
pinch of salt
4 tablespoons extra virgin olive oil

Photograph opposite

Preheat the oven to 350°F/180°C/Gas Mark 4 and line a roasting pan with parchment paper.

Drain the anchovies, pat dry using paper towels, and coarsely chop. Wash and dry 1 orange and remove the zest with a peeler. Bring a small pan of water to a boil, add the orange zest, and blanch for 5 minutes, then drain and finely chop. Mix the anchovies, orange zest, and chopped parsley together in a bowl.

Squeeze the remaining orange and strain the juice, then set aside with the orange shell.

Lightly season the veal with salt, then spread the anchovy mixture on top. Wrap each veal slice in pancetta and tie with kitchen twine. Transfer the veal to the prepared roasting pan and pour the strained orange juice over the meat. Add the chopped rosemary, black pepper, some zest from the second orange and cook in the oven for 20 minutes. Turn on the broiler (grill) and cook for another 5 minutes.

Meanwhile, put the salad greens (leaves) and herbs into a salad bowl. Mix the vinegar, salt, and oil together and drizzle it over the leaves. Serve alongside the meat.

Arrosto al limone

Braised Veal with Lemon

Serves 4
Preparation: 15 minutes,
    plus 3 hours marinating
Cooking: 1 hour 10 minutes

6 tablespoons olive oil
juice of 1 lemon, strained
1 x 1¾-lb/800-g veal round
    (topside)
salt and pepper

Beat the olive oil and lemon juice together in a large dish, season with salt and pepper, and add the veal, turning to coat. Let marinate, turning occasionally, for 3 hours.

Transfer the veal and the marinade to a large pan, pour in ⅔ cup (5 fl oz/150 ml) water, and bring to a boil. Once boiling, reduce the heat and simmer for about 1 hour, or until tender. Remove the veal from the pan, carve into slices, and place in a warm serving dish. Boil the cooking juices until slightly reduced, then pour into a sauceboat and serve with the veal.

Lamb

Lamb, *agnello* in Italian, might not be the meat that first comes to mind when most people of other nations think of Italian food. Hams, beef ragù, veal saltimbocca, and even wild boar are more common. But Italy is diverse, mountainous, and green as well as arid and coastal, alpine as well as Mediterranean, and the *cucine* of Italy, which became one country only 150 years ago, are rich in their use of lamb.

Italian *cucina*, however, is one in its respect for ingredients and flavor—nothing is wasted, and every ingredient is used to maximum effect. If you buy the best-quality lamb you can, the following recipes will bring the best out of it. The cuts of lamb stated in the following recipes are the cuts that would be used in Italy, and what will be available to buy, so if you buy the stated cuts you can use them according to the recipes with confidence—you can ask your butcher to remove the bone or trim the fat if that's a bridge too far for you.

Milk-fed lamb is an animal that's been fed only by its mother when it comes to slaughter. *Abbachio* is the Italian name for five- to six-week-old lamb, popular in the Lazio region. If it's labeled "lamb" in the United States, it's usually six to eight months old, and no older than a year. There's no need to worry; it will be young and mild enough in flavor to be used in any Italian recipe that calls for lamb, and will need cooking for only slightly longer than the recipe states if you're substituting it for milk-fed (another five minutes) or another ten minutes for *abbachio*. This is because animals that graze, and therefore range, have better developed muscles that those that have been fed on only milk, and so they will need longer cooking to break down their more developed muscle tissue. Mutton is more than a year old and has a richer, gamier flavor and needs longer cooking still. It's a niche meat in the United States, so if you do find some, and you want to try it in a recipe, don't cook a large batch if it's your first encounter. It will take a lot longer to cook, and can still be quite chewy, so be prepared.

Lamb is a rather fatty meat and will shrink as a result of that fat melting and the muscles contracting when you cook it, so you will need to buy a little more than you would do of an equivalent amount of beef or pork. But the recipes that follow take this into account, so follow them exactly.

Roasting cuts

Leg is an excellent cut to feed a crowd; shoulder costs less, is fattier, and will take longer. Saddle is an impressive, lean, expensive cut that will serve eight to ten people. Loin is fattier than leg but less so than shoulder and is excellent for stuffing when boned, as is breast, which is the fattiest joint but inexpensive. Rack of lamb or best end of neck is the choicest, most expensive cut and is lean, so it will cook fast, and will serve two people, as will chump (where the loin meets the leg), which is inexpensive and boneless.

Stewing and braising cuts

Any part of the lamb can be stewed or braised well, cut into chunks, but it is sensible to use less expensive cuts, such as neck (scrag end), which is tough, but tastes great when cooked for a long time, or shanks, which become really tender with long, slow cooking. Shoulder needs to be trimmed of fat first, and skimmed as you cook, but gives great results, and chump provides great flavor when diced and cooked long and slow.

Italian cuts and cooking techniques

1 Collo
Stewing and braising

2 Spalla
Roasting and stewing

3 Carré
Ideal for broiling (grilling)

4 Petto
Suitable for stews

5 Sella
Excellent for roasting

6 Cosciotto
The best part for roasting

American cuts and cooking techniques

1 Neck slices
Stewing

2 Shoulder
Roasting, stewing, and cut into chops for broiling (grilling) and frying

3 Rib
Roasting, and cut into chops for broiling (grilling) and frying

4 Loin
Roasting, and cut into chops for broiling (grilling) and frying

5 Leg
Roasting, and cut into chops for broiling (grilling) and frying

6 Hind shank
Braising and ground (minced) meat

7 Breast
Boned and rolled for roasting and ground (minced) meat

8 Foreshank
Braising and ground (minced) meat

British cuts and cooking techniques

1 Scrag end of neck
Stewing and braising

2 Middle neck
Stewing and casseroles

3 Shoulder
Roasting, barbecues, kebabs, casseroles

4 Foreshank
Braising

5 Best end of neck
(Also known as rack of lamb). Roasting, and cut into chops for broiling (grilling) and stewing

6 Loin
Roasting, including whole saddle, and cut into chops for broiling (grilling) or frying, into fillet or into noisettes

7 Chump
Roasting, and cut into leg chops for broiling (grilling) and stewing

8 Leg
Roasting, and cut into leg chops for broiling (grilling)

9 Hind shank
Braising

10 Breast
Boned and rolled for roasting or braising

Cosciotto d'agnello con radici al forno

Roasted Leg of Lamb with Root Vegetables

Serves 4
Preparation: 30 minutes
Cooking: 1 hour 20 minutes,
   plus 10 minutes resting

1 x 4½-lb/2-kg leg of lamb
6 cloves garlic
2 oz/50 g pancetta
2 sprigs rosemary, leaves only
4–5 tablespoons extra virgin
   olive oil
⅔ cup (5 fl oz/150 ml) white wine
4 carrots, cut into large chunks
2 sweet potatoes, sliced
2 turnips, sliced
salt and pepper

Preheat the oven to 325°F/160°C/Gas Mark 3. Using a small knife, make several deep incisions into the lamb. Finely chop one of the garlic cloves with the pancetta and rosemary leaves. Insert the chopped ingredients deep into the incisions, then rub the meat with a pinch of salt and a grind of pepper and tie with kitchen twine.

Pour the olive oil into a roasting pan, add the remaining garlic cloves, the wine, ⅔ cup (5 fl oz/150 ml) warm water, and the lamb. Roast in the oven for 1 hour, basting occasionally with the cooking juices.

Meanwhile, bring a pan of salted water to a boil and blanch the root vegetables separately for 5–6 minutes, then drain.

Increase the oven temperature to 350°F/180°C/Gas Mark 4 and add the vegetables to the roasting pan, season with salt, if necessary, and mix the vegetables with the cooking juices. Cook for another 20 minutes, basting the meat occasionally with the cooking juices.

Once cooked, remove the lamb from the pan, cover with kitchen foil, and rest for 10 minutes. Carve the meat into slices and place in a serving dish. Drizzle with the cooking juices and serve with the root vegetables.

Note: Calculate the cooking time of the lamb based on the weight of the meat. After the initial searing, the cooking time for rare to medium-rare is 10 minutes for every 1 lb 2 oz/500 g. For medium or well-done lamb, 12 minutes and 20 minutes are needed respectively.

Cosciotto arrosto
Roasted Leg of Lamb

Serves 6
Preparation: 20 minutes
Cooking: 1½ hours, plus
   10 minutes resting

butter, for greasing
1 x 4½ lb/2 kg leg of lamb
3 oz/80 g pancetta, cut into strips
6 fresh sage leaves, cut into strips
1 tablespoon rosemary
olive oil, for brushing
4 garlic cloves, chopped
5 tablespoons white wine vinegar
5 tablespoons white wine
salt and pepper
baby spinach, to serve

Photograph page 121

Preheat the oven to 200°C/400°F/Gas Mark 6. Grease a roasting pan with the butter. Wrap the lamb with the strips of pancetta and, using a small, pointed knife, make small incisions all over it. Insert the sage and some of the rosemary into the incisions. Brush the lamb all over with oil, place in the prepared roasting pan, and season with salt and pepper. Sprinkle the garlic and remaining rosemary on top, pour in the vinegar and wine, and roast for 1½ hours. Turn the lamb halfway through the cooking time and baste occasionally with the cooking juices.

Remove the lamb from the roasting pan, cover with kitchen foil, and let rest for 10 minutes. Carve the meat and place in a warm serving dish. Serve with a salad of baby spinach.

Cosciotto in crosta d'erbe
Roasted Leg of Lamb in a Herb Crust

Serves 6
Preparation: 25 minutes
Cooking: 1½ hours, plus
   10 minutes resting

2 tablespoons chopped thyme
2 tablespoons chopped oregano
2 tablespoons chopped flat-leaf
   parsley
2 tablespoons chopped rosemary
4 tablespoons olive oil
1½ cups (2¾ oz/70 g) fresh
   bread crumbs
1 x 4½-lb/2-kg leg of lamb
salt and pepper

Photograph opposite

Preheat the oven to 475°F/240°C/Gas Mark 9. Combine the thyme, oregano, parsley, and rosemary in a bowl, add the oil and bread crumbs, season with salt and pepper, and mix well.

Put the lamb into a large roasting pan, spread the herb mixture over it, and roast for 15 minutes. Reduce the oven temperature to 350°F/180°C/Gas Mark 4, add ⅔ cup (5 fl oz/150 ml) warm water to the roasting pan, and roast for another 1¼ hours, or until tender.

Remove the lamb from the roasting pan, cover with kitchen foil, and let rest for 10 minutes. Carve the meat and place in a warm serving dish. Serve.

Note: For a side dish, halve and seed some tomatoes, fill with bread crumbs and chopped oregano, drizzle with olive oil, season with salt and pepper, and bake for 15 minutes.

Loin of Lamb with Garlic and Fennel Seeds

Serves 4
Preparation: 15 minutes
Cooking: 1 hour

1 tablespoon fennel seeds
few black peppercorns
pinch of kosher or coarse salt
1 loin of lamb, bones left in
6–7 tablespoons extra virgin
   olive oil
4 bulbs garlic
¼ cup (2 fl oz/60 ml) Cognac
1 baguette, sliced and toasted

For the salad:
mixed greens (salad leaves)
olive oil, to taste
lemon juice, to taste
salt

Photograph opposite

Preheat the oven to 350°F/180°C/Gas Mark 4. Blend the fennel seeds with the black peppercorns and kosher or coarse salt in a small food processor. (Alternatively, grind the ingredients in a mortar with a pestle.) Brush the lamb with 1 tablespoon of the olive oil, then spread the mixture evenly over the meat and cover the bones with small strips of kitchen foil.

Transfer the lamb to a roasting pan with the remaining oil and the garlic bulbs and cook in the oven for 15 minutes. Pour the Cognac over the meat, add a ladleful of hot water to the bottom of the pan, and cook for another 40–45 minutes.

Remove the meat from the roasting pan and wrap in foil to keep warm. Open the garlic bulbs carefully so as not to burn yourself and squeeze the pulp into the cooking juices. Blend with a handheld blender until it is a smooth, creamy consistency. Spread the mixture on a few slices of the toasted bread.

Dress the mixed salad greens (leaves) with oil, lemon juice, and salt. Serve the lamb with the toasted bread and the salad on the side.

Note: To intensify the flavor of the fennel seeds, substitute Cognac with ¼ cup (2 fl oz/60 ml) Pernod or another anise liqueur. If you prefer your meat well done, cook the lamb for an extra 10 minutes.

Agnello all'acciuga con scalogni

Lamb with Anchovies and Shallots

Serves 4
Preparation: 30 minutes,
   plus 20 minutes soaking
Cooking: 2 hours 40 minutes

1 tablespoon salted capers
4 salted anchovies
1 clove garlic, peeled
1 x 2½-lb/1.2-kg leg of lamb, boned
1 heaping teaspoon dried herbes
   de Provence
1 tablespoon extra virgin olive oil
⅔ cup (5 fl oz/150 ml) white wine
12 shallots, peeled
1¼ tablespoons all-purpose
   (plain) flour
scant 1 cup (7 fl oz/200 ml)
   vegetable broth (stock)
salt and pepper

Soak the capers in a small bowl of lukewarm water for 20 minutes. Wash the anchovies under running water to remove the salt and soak in a small bowl of water for 10 minutes. Drain the anchovies, bone, rinse, and dry. Drain and rinse the capers and chop along with the anchovies and garlic.

Preheat the oven to 275°F/140°C/Gas Mark 1. Using a sharp knife, open the leg of lamb and rub the chopped ingredients inside. Close and tie with kitchen twine. Mix the herbes de Provence with a pinch of salt, a grind of pepper, and the olive oil, and rub onto the lamb. Place the lamb in a roasting pan on the stove (hob) and sear over high heat, turning until browned on all sides. Pour the wine over the lamb and cover with kitchen foil. Cook in the oven for 2 hours.

Bring a pan of salted water to a boil, add the peeled shallots, and blanch for 5 minutes. Drain and arrange around the meat. Increase the oven temperature to 400°F/200°C/Gas Mark 6 and cook for another 20 minutes, basting the meat with the cooking juices. Remove the meat and shallots from the oven and keep warm.

Sprinkle the cooking juices with the flour, pour in the broth (stock), and stir with a whisk. Cook the sauce over low heat for 7–8 minutes, then add the shallots, warm for 2–3 minutes, and serve with the carved meat.

Note: The leg of lamb may be substituted with a boned lamb shoulder. This can be served with a side dish of 14 oz/400 g new potatoes. Wash the potatoes, blanch in a pan of boiling salted water for 5 minutes, and cook together with the shallots.

Carré farcito alle verdure

Loin of Lamb Stuffed with Vegetables

Serves 6
Preparation: 40 minutes
Cooking: 1 hour, plus 10 minutes
**   resting**

4 tablespoons olive oil
1 loin of lamb, excess fat removed
    and set aside
1 small eggplant (aubergine),
    finely diced
1 zucchini (courgette), finely diced
¼ bell pepper, finely diced
2 tablespoons heavy (double)
    cream
1 egg yolk
1 teaspoon chopped thyme
1 teaspoon chopped marjoram
½ cup (1 oz/25 g) fresh
    bread crumbs, to sprinkle
1 piece pork caul fat
few drops balsamic vinegar
salt and pepper

Preheat the oven to 400°F/200°C/Gas Mark 6. Line a roasting pan with baking parchment and oil the parchment with 2 tablespoons of the oil.

Using a sharp knife, make an incision lengthwise down the lamb, (not going all the way through the meat) to create a pocket.

Heat the remaining oil in a skillet (frying pan) over medium heat and add the eggplant (aubergine), zucchini (courgette), and bell pepper. Season with salt and pepper and sauté for 5 minutes, or until tender.

Put the excess lamb fat, the sautéed vegetables, the cream, egg yolk, thyme, and marjoram into a food processor and process until smooth. Season with salt and pepper. Use the mixture to stuff the lamb pocket, then sew the pocket closed with a trussing needle and thick white thread. Sprinkle the meat with fresh breadcrumbs and season with salt and pepper. Wrap the lamb in the caul fat and tie with kitchen twine.

In a hot skillet, sear the lamb wrapped in caul fat on all sides over high heat, then put into the prepared roasting pan. Cook in the oven for 35 minutes for pinker meat or 45 minutes if you prefer the lamb to be well done. Baste the meat regularly with the cooking juices. Add a little not water if the roasting pan starts to dry out.

Remove the lamb from the oven and rest for 10 minutes. Remove the kitchen twine, carve the stuffed meat into slices and arrange in a warm serving dish. Drizzle with a few drops of balsamic vinegar and the cooking juices, and serve.

Note: If you can't find a whole loin of lamb, a good alternative is a boneless saddle of lamb. There is no need to make an incision in the meat to create a pocket, because there is already a cavity between the two loins. Add the ½ cup (1 oz/25 g) fresh bread crumbs to the stuffing mixture. You won't need the caul fat; simply wrap the meat around the mixture so it overlaps and tie with kitchen twine.

Cosciotto d'agnello con pancetta e feta

Leg of Lamb with Pancetta and Feta Cheese

Serves 6
Preparation: 15 minutes,
  plus 2 hours standing
Cooking: 40 minutes, plus
  10 minutes resting

1 x 4½-lb/2-kg leg of lamb
1 onion, sliced
1 cup (5 oz/150 g) feta cheese
1 tablespoon chopped thyme
grated zest of 1 unwaxed lemon
3½ oz/100 g slices (rashers)
  pancetta
4–5 tablespoons olive oil
⅔ cup (5 fl oz/150 ml) white wine
salt and pepper

For the marinade:
1¼ cups (11 oz/300 g) plain yogurt
1 clove garlic
4–5 juniper berries, crushed
1 bay leaf, shredded

Mix the yogurt, garlic, crushed juniper berries, and shredded bay leaf in a large ovenproof dish with a pinch of salt and a grind of pepper. Add the lamb and rub with the mixture, then rest for 2 hours in the refrigerator.

Preheat the oven to 350°F/180°C/Gas Mark 4. In a bowl, break up the feta with a fork and mix with the thyme and grated lemon zest.

Remove the lamb from the marinade and drain. Discard the marinade. Cover the lamb with the feta mixture and wrap in the pancetta. Tie the lamb with kitchen twine, then place in a roasting pan with the oil and wine, and roast in the oven for 40 minutes, basting occasionally with the cooking juices. Add a small ladleful of warm water if the pan starts to dry out.

Remove the lamb from the pan, cover with kitchen foil, and rest for 10 minutes. Carve the lamb into slices and serve with its cooking juices.

Note: The feta can be replaced with a medium goat cheese, and the grated lemon zest with the grated zest of an unwaxed orange. The dish also works well when served with a pea purée (see page 262).

Loin of Lamb with Thyme and Escarole

Serves 6
Preparation: 20 minutes
Cooking: 1 hour 55 minutes

4 tablespoons olive oil
1 loin of lamb, boned and bones
   set aside, then meat thickly
   sliced
3 stalks celery, diced
3 carrots, diced
2 onions, diced
grated zest of 2 lemons
⅔ cup (5 fl oz/150 ml) dry
   white wine
2 egg yolks
scant ¼ cup (1¾ fl oz/50 ml)
   heavy (double) cream
4 tablespoons butter, plus
   a pat (knob)
1 tablespoon chopped thyme
1 tablespoon chopped parsley
2¼ lb/1 kg escarole
salt and pepper

Photograph opposite

Preheat the oven to 425°F/220°C/Gas Mark 7. Line a roasting pan with baking parchment and oil the parchment with 1 tablespoon of the oil.

Heat the remaining oil in a heavy pan. Add the bones, diced celery, carrots, and onions, and the lemon zest and cook over medium heat until the vegetables are browned on all sides. Add the wine and let evaporate. Pour in enough cold water to cover and bring to a boil. Reduce the heat and cook until the liquid has reduced by half. Remove the lamb bones from the pan and set aside.

Strain the mixture through a strainer (sieve) into a small saucepan. While stirring quickly, mix in the egg yolks and cream. Season with salt and pepper, and heat over low heat.

Meanwhile, mix the 4 tablespoons of butter with the thyme and parsley in a small bowl. Spread the mixture over the slices of lamb, season with salt and pepper, and place the meat in the prepared roasting pan. Cook in the oven for about 20 minutes, or until tender.

While the meat is cooking, bring a pan of salted water to a boil, add the escarole, and blanch for 4–5 minutes, then drain and let cool. Heat the pat (knob) of butter in a skillet (frying pan) over medium heat, shake off any excess water from the escarole, and sauté with a pinch of salt for about 10 minutes, or until tender.

Serve the lamb with the sauce and escarole on the side.

Spalla al cartoccio

Lamb Shoulder in a Package

Serves 6
Preparation: 30 minutes
Cooking: 1 hour

olive oil, for brushing
1 x 2¼-lb/1-kg boneless lamb
   shoulder, trimmed of fat
1 sprig flat-leaf parsley, chopped
1 sprig chervil, chopped
1 sprig oregano, chopped
1 bay leaf
¾ cup (6 fl oz/175 ml)
   dry white wine
juice of ½ lemon, strained
salt and pepper

Photograph opposite

Preheat the oven to 400°F/200°C/Gas Mark 6. Place a large sheet of parchment paper on a baking sheet and brush generously with olive oil. Season the top and underside of the lamb with salt and pepper and place it in the middle of the oiled parchment paper. Sprinkle with the chopped herbs and add the bay leaf. Holding up all sides of the parchment paper, slowly pour the wine and lemon juice on top and wrap the paper carefully so that the liquid does not leak out. Roast in the oven for 1 hour, or until cooked through and tender. Open the package slightly to let the steam escape, then serve.

◆

Fricassea con cipolline

Lamb Fricassée with Onions

Serves 4
Preparation: 20 minutes
Cooking: 1 hour

3 tablespoons butter
3 tablespoons olive oil
1 x 1¾-lb/800-g leg of lamb,
   chopped into fairly small
   pieces (you can ask your
   butcher to do this for you)
14 oz/400 g pearl (baby) onions
2¼ cups (17 fl oz/500 ml)
   dry white wine
2 egg yolks
juice of 1 lemon, strained
salt and pepper

Heat the butter and oil in a large pan, add the pieces of lamb, and cook over high heat, turning frequently, for about 10 minutes or until golden brown all over. Remove the lamb from the pan, set aside, and keep warm.

Add the onions to the pan and cook over medium heat, stirring frequently, for about 10 minutes, or until golden brown. Return the pieces of lamb to the pan, season with salt and pepper, and pour in the wine. Cover and cook over medium heat for 40 minutes.

Beat the egg yolks with the lemon juice in a bowl. Move the pan to the edge of the stove (hob) and pour in the egg yolk mixture. Stir quickly so that the mixture thickens and coats the pieces of lamb without drying out. Transfer to a warm serving dish and serve.

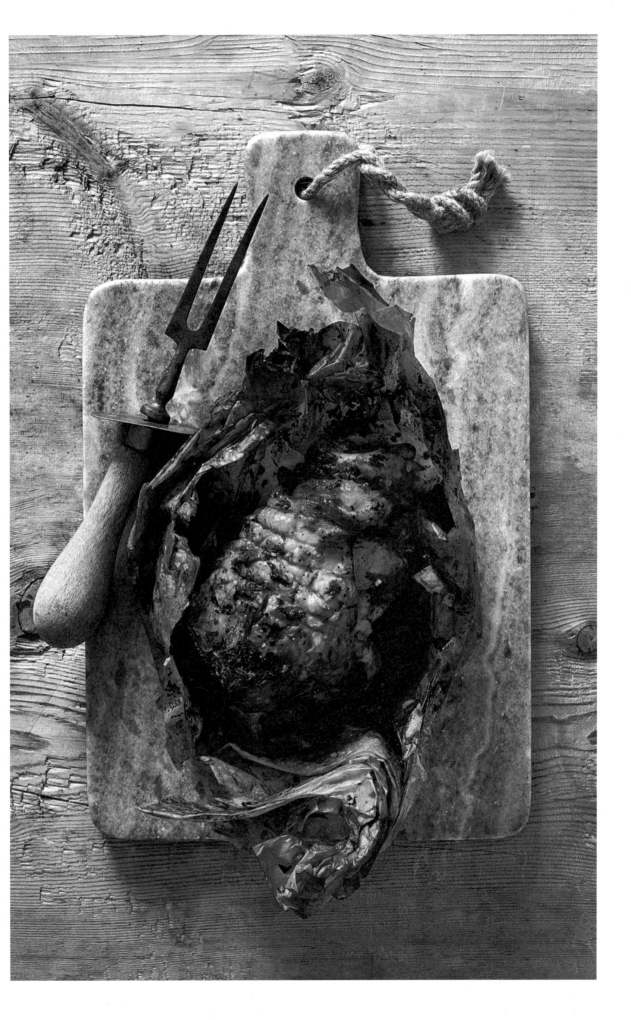

Cosciotto alla cacciatora

Cacciatore-Style Leg of Lamb

Serves 4
Preparation: 25 minutes,
    plus 12 hours marinating
Cooking: 2 hours

1 x 3-/b/1.4-kg leg of lamb
3 tablespoons olive oil

For the marinade:
1 tablespoon olive oil
1 clove garlic, chopped
1 shallot, chopped
1 onion, chopped
½ carrot, chopped
1¼ cups (10 fl oz/300 ml) red wine
½ cup (4 fl oz/120 ml) red wine
    vinegar
¼ cup (2 fl oz/60 ml) grappa
1 slice lemon
3 juniper berries
1 clove
5 black peppercorns
salt

For the sauce:
2 tablespoons butter
1 shallot, chopped
1 tablespoon chopped onion
scant ¼ cup (1 oz/25 g) all-purpose
    (plain) flour
generous 1 cup (9 fl oz/275 ml)
    meat broth (stock)
1 tablespoon chopped parsley

The day before, prepare the marinade. Heat the oil in a saucepan, add the garlic and shallot, and cook for a few minutes until golden. Add the remaining ingredients to the pan and cook over low heat for 10 minutes. Remove from the heat and let cool.

Slash the leg of lamb so that the marinade can penetrate the meat. Place it in a large dish, pour over the cooled marinade, and cover with plastic wrap (clingfilm). Let marinate in the refrigerator for 12 hours, turning occasionally.

The next day, preheat the oven to 400°F/200°C/Gas Mark 6. Remove the lamb from the marinade, reserving the marinade, and pat the lamb dry with paper towels, then brush with the oil. Place the lamb on a broiler (grill) rack set in a roasting pan and pour 1 cup (8 fl oz/ 250 ml) water into the roasting pan. Cook in the oven for 20 minutes. Reduce the oven temperature to 350°F/180°C/Gas Mark 4 and cook for another 40 minutes, basting the meat regularly. Keep pouring a little water into the pan regularly so it doesn't dry out.

Meanwhile to prepare the sauce, pour generous 1 cup (9 fl oz/ 275 ml) strained marinade into a pan and cook over medium-low heat until it is reduced by half. Melt the butter in another saucepan, add the chopped shallot and onion, and sauté for 5 minutes, or until browned. Mix in the flour and cook until colored, then add the reduced marinade, the broth (stock), and parsley and cook over low heat for 15 minutes.

Remove the lamb from the oven, carve into slices, and serve with the sauce on the side.

Abbacchio all giudia

Jewish-Style Suckling Lamb

Serves 6
Preparation: 30 minutes
Cooking: 50 minutes, plus
    5 minutes resting

scant ¼ cup (1½ oz/40 g) lard
½ onion, finely chopped
2 oz/50 g prosciutto crudo,
    finely chopped
1 x 2¼-lb/1-kg suckling lamb,
    cut into medium chunks,
    rinsed, and patted dry
½ tablespoon all-purpose
    (plain) flour
½ cup (4 fl oz/120 ml) white wine
3 egg yolks
1 sprig parsley, chopped
pinch of dried marjoram
juice of 1 lemon
salt and pepper

Melt the lard in a large pan over low heat, add the onion and prosciutto, and brown gently. Add the lamb, season with salt and pepper, and cook over high heat until the meat is browned all over. Sprinkle the meat with the flour and stir. After 2 minutes, pour in the wine and let evaporate. Add a ladleful of hot water to the pan, cover with a lid, and cook for 40–45 minutes, stirring occasionally and adding more hot water if the pan starts to dry out.

Meanwhile, beat the egg yolks, parsley, marjoram, and lemon juice together in a bowl. One minute before the end of the cooking time, pour the mixture into the pan and stir rapidly to evenly distribute the mixture.

Remove the pan from the heat, cover, and set aside to rest for 5 minutes, or until it the sauce is a creamy consistency. Transfer to a warm serving dish and serve.

Agnello alla Mauritana

Mauritania-Style Lamb

Serves 4
Preparation: 25 minutes
Cooking: 1½ hours

6 tablespoons olive oil
1 x 2¼-lb/1-kg lamb, cut into
    chunks, rinsed, and patted dry
1 white onion, finely chopped
2¼ cups (9 oz/250 g) sun-dried
    tomatoes, finely chopped
2 cups (11 oz/300 g) fregula or
    Israeli or pearl (giant) couscous
salt and pepper

Heat the oil in a large saucepan over high heat, add the lamb, and cook until the meat is browned all over. Add the onion and sun-dried tomatoes, stir, and cook for 1 hour. Season moderately with salt and pepper, remove the stewed meat from the pan, cover, and set aside in a warm place.

Pour about 4¼ cups (34 fl oz/1 liter) water into the saucepan with the cooking juices. Bring to a boil and add the fregula or Israeli or pearl (giant) couscous, stirring continuously. Reduce the heat and cook, uncovered, for 10 minutes, or until the water has evaporated completely. Make sure the fregula does not dry out.

Transfer the fregula or couscous to a warm serving dish, arrange the stewed lamb on top, and serve.

Agnello all'Abruzzese
Abruzzo-Style Lamb

Serves 4
Preparation: 20 minutes
Cooking: 1¼ hours

3 tablespoons olive oil
3 oz/80 g pancetta, diced
1 x 2½-lb/1.2-kg leg of lamb,
    meat only, chopped
1 onion, coarsely chopped
1 carrot, coarsely chopped
1 stalk celery, coarsely chopped
½ cup (120 ml/4 fl oz) white wine
scant 2½ cups (14 oz/400 g)
    chopped tomatoes
pinch of oregano
1 tablespoon chopped parsley,
    plus extra to garnish
salt and pepper

Photograph opposite

Heat the oil in a large lidded skillet (frying pan) over high heat, add the diced pancetta, followed by the lamb, and cook until the meat is golden brown all over. Add the chopped onion, carrot, and celery, stir, and season with salt and pepper. Pour in the white wine and let evaporate. Pass the chopped tomatoes through a strainer (sieve) and add to the meat with the oregano and parsley. Cover and cook over medium heat for 1 hour, stirring occasionally.

Remove the lamb from the skillet and keep warm. Pour the sauce into a blender or food processor and blend until smooth. Serve the lamb dressed with the sauce and sprinkled with chopped parsley.

Agnello alle erbe aromatiche
Lamb with Aromatic Herbs

Serves 6
Preparation: 30 minutes, plus
    15 minutes
Cooking: 1¼ hours

⅔ cup (5 fl oz/150 ml) vinegar
2 sprigs rosemary, chopped
2–3 sage leaves
2–3 bay leaves
1 lb 2 oz/500 g (about 4) tomatoes
1 x 3¼-lb/1.5-kg lamb shoulder,
    cut into medium chunks,
    rinsed, and dried
all-purpose (plain) flour, for dusting
3–4 tablespoons olive oil
1 clove garlic
2–3 anchovy fillets
salt and pepper

Pour the vinegar into a bowl, add the chopped rosemary, sage, and bay leaves, and let infuse for 15 minutes.

Plunge the tomatoes first into a heatproof bowl of hot water, then transfer to a bowl of cold water, drain, and remove the skins and seeds. Dice the tomato flesh and set aside.

Dust the lamb with flour, put into a colander, and shake off any excess. Heat the oil in a flameproof Dutch oven (casserole), add the garlic, and fry for 1–2 minutes, or until golden brown. Remove the garlic, add the anchovy fillets, and heat until dissolved. Add the lamb and brown well on all sides. Pour the herb-infused vinegar over the meat, let evaporate, and season with salt and pepper. Add the diced tomatoes to the lamb, cover with the lid, and cook for 1 hour, stirring occasionally. Season with salt and pepper.

Remove the lamb from the heat, transfer to a large warm serving dish, and serve.

Fricassea ai carciofi

Lamb Fricassee with Artichokes

Serves 4
Preparation: 20 minutes
Cooking: 1 hour 10 minutes

2 tablespoons olive oil
½ onion, chopped
½ carrot, chopped
½ stalk celery, chopped
1 clove garlic, chopped
1¾ lb/800 g lamb shoulder, cut
  into pieces
1 tablespoon all-purpose
  (plain) flour
½ cup (4 fl oz/120 ml) white wine
4 artichokes hearts, quartered
2 eggs
juice of 1 lemon
1 sprig parsley, chopped
salt and pepper

Heat the oil in a flameproof Dutch oven (casserole) over medium heat. Add the chopped vegetables and garlic cook for 5 minutes before adding the lamb. Sprinkle the meat with the flour and cook until browned. Add the wine, let evaporate, and cook for 40 minutes. Season with salt and pepper. Remove the meat from the Dutch oven and set aside.

Add the artichoke hearts to the Dutch oven and cook for 20 minutes. Return the meat to the Dutch oven and cook for another 5 minutes.

Meanwhile, whisk together the eggs, lemon juice, and chopped parsley in a bowl. Just before serving, pour the sauce over the lamb and mix quickly. The egg mixture should just cover the lamb. Remove from the heat immediately so that the eggs do not curdle, and serve.

Note: If you like the taste of pepper, add a generous grind to the beaten eggs together with some chopped marjoram.

Agnello alla maremmana

Maremma-Style Lamb

Serves 4
Preparation: 15 minutes
Cooking time: 45 minutes

2 tablespoons olive oil
1 onion, chopped
1 clove garlic, chopped
1¾ lb/800 g lamb, cut into chunks
3 ripe tomatoes, coarsely chopped
2 bell peppers, cored, seeded,
  and cut into thin strips
6-8 sage leaves, ½ chopped
½ cup (4 fl oz/120 ml) dry white
  wine
1 tablespoon all-purpose
  (plain) flour
salt and pepper

Photograph opposite

Heat the oil in a pan over medium heat, add the onion and garlic, and lightly sauté for a few minutes, then add the lamb and cook for 10 minutes, or until browned all over. Add the chopped tomatoes, strips of bell pepper, and sage leaves, reserving a few to garnish. Season with salt and pepper and mix well. Pour in the wine and let evaporate. Sprinkle the meat with the flour and stir well. Add 2 ladlefuls of boiling water to dilute the cooking juices, cover, and cook over medium heat for 30 minutes. Garnish with the reserved sage leaves and serve.

Abbacchio alla romana
Roman Spring Lamb

Serves 4
Preparation: 30 minutes
Cooking: 50 minutes

1 x 2¼-lb/1-kg leg of lamb
all-purpose (plain) flour, for dusting
3 tablespoons olive oil
3 sprigs rosemary
4 sage leaves, chopped
1 clove garlic, crushed
¾ cup (6 fl oz/175 ml) white wine
5 tablespoons white wine vinegar,
    plus extra as needed
4 potatoes, sliced
salt and pepper

Photograph opposite

Chop the lamb meat into pieces or ask the butcher to do this for you. Preheat the oven to 350°F/180°C/Gas Mark 4.

Dust the meat with flour, put into a colander, and shake off any excess. Heat the oil in a large, wide roasting pan (with a lid), add the lamb, and cook on the stove (hob) over high heat, turning frequently, for about 10 minutes, or until browned all over. Season with salt and pepper, add the rosemary sprigs, and sprinkle with the chopped sage and crushed garlic. Turn the pieces over several times so that they soak up the flavors.

Combine the wine and vinegar in a bowl, add to the roasting pan, and cook until the liquid has almost completely evaporated. Pour in ⅔ cup (5 fl oz/150 ml) boiling water, add the potatoes, and stir. Cover and roast in the oven for 30 minutes, or until tender. If the gravy seems to be drying out, add a little hot water mixed with white wine vinegar. Transfer the lamb to a warm serving dish and serve.

Note: Alternatively, omit the potatoes, and, when the lamb is nearly ready, transfer 2–3 tablespoons of the pan juices to a small pan, add 3 salted anchovies, boned and chopped, and cook over low heat, mashing the anchovies with a wooden spoon until they have almost dissolved. Mix well, pour the sauce over the meat, and roast for an additional few minutes before serving.

Agnello e cicoria
Lamb and Chicory

Serves 4
Preparation: 10 minutes
Cooking: 1¼ hours

2¼ lb/1 kg chicory or endive
   (preferably wild)
scant ½ cup (3½ fl oz/100 ml)
   olive oil
4 cloves garlic, crushed
2¼ lb/1 kg lamb, cut into chunks
scant ½ cup (3½ fl oz/100 ml)
   dry white wine
4 eggs
3½ oz/100 g pecorino cheese,
   grated (about 1⅓ cups)
salt and pepper

Bring a large saucepan of salted water to a boil, add the chicory or endive, and boil for about 15 minutes, or until tender. Drain, chop finely, and set aside.

Heat the oil in a large flameproof Dutch oven (casserole), add the crushed garlic, and fry for a few seconds until golden brown. Add the lamb and sear over high heat until browned all over. Pour in the wine and let evaporate. Season with salt and pepper, reduce the heat to low, and cook for 45 minutes, or until the lamb is cooked. Add the chicory and keep over the heat for another few minutes.

Five minutes before the end of the cooking time, beat the eggs and cheese together in a bowl. Pour the egg mixture over the lamb, stir rapidly, and cook over low heat for a few minutes or until the egg mixture has formed a creamy film around the meat. Transfer to a warm serving dish and serve.

Agnello al finocchietto
Lamb with Wild Fennel

Serves 6
Preparation: 30 minutes
Cooking: 1 hour 30 minutes

2¼ lb/1 kg lamb, cut into
   medium chunks, rinsed, and
   patted dry
all-purpose (plain) flour, for dusting
⅔ cup (5 fl oz/150 ml) olive oil
1 onion, chopped
9 oz/250 g peeled tomatoes,
   passed through a strainer
   (sieve) or 1 tablespoon tomato
   paste (purée), diluted with
   a little warm water
2¼ lb/1 kg wild fennel
salt and pepper

Season the lamb chunks with salt and pepper. Dust with flour, put into a colander, and shake off any excess. Heat the oil in a large, deep skillet (frying pan), add the meat, and sear over high heat for about 5 minutes, or until browned all over. Do this in batches if necessary. Reduce the heat to medium, add the onion, and sauté for about 5 minutes, or until browned. Add the strained, peeled tomatoes or the diluted tomato paste (purée), stir, and continue to cook over medium heat stirring occasionally.

Meanwhile, pour 2¼ cups (17 fl oz/500 ml) water into a flameproof Dutch oven (casserole). Place over high heat, add the wild fennel, and boil for 10 minutes. Drain and set aside, reserving the water.

Pour the fennel cooking water into the skillet, season with salt and pepper, and cook for 50 minutes. Add a little water every now and then if the skillet starts to dry out. Ten minutes before the end of the cooking time, add the boiled fennel. Remove from the heat, transfer to a warm serving dish, and serve.

Agnello del pastore
Shepherd's-Style Lamb

Serves 6
Preparation: 30 minutes, plus
3–4 hours marinating
Cooking: 1 hour 20 minutes

3¼ lb/1.5 kg lamb or 2¼ lb/1 kg
veal, cut into large chunks,
rinsed, and dried
2 cloves garlic, sliced
olive oil, for drizzling
2 tablespoons lard
2 onions, thinly sliced
11 oz/300 g pecorino cheese,
thinly sliced
salt and pepper

Put the meat into a large flameproof Dutch oven (casserole) and season with salt and pepper. Sprinkle the sliced garlic on top, drizzle with plenty of oil, and let marinate for 3–4 hours in the refrigerator.

When ready to cook, preheat the oven to 350°F/180°C/Gas Mark 4. Melt the lard in a roasting pan over medium heat, add the onions, and sauté for 5 minutes, or until the onion is soft and translucent, then remove from the pan and set aside.

Increase the heat to high, add the meat to the pan and sear for about 5 minutes, or until browned all over. Pour in ½ cup (4 fl oz/ 120 ml) water and cover with the pecorino cheese. Sprinkle the onions on top, cover with a lid, and cook in the oven for 1 hour. Remove from the oven and serve.

Agnello cacio e uova
Lamb with Sheep Cheese and Eggs

Serves 4–6
Preparation: 20 minutes
Cooking: 25 minutes

4 tablespoons olive oil
3 cloves garlic
3¼ lb/1.5 kg lamb, cut into
small bite-size chunks,
rinsed, and patted dry
⅔ cup (5 fl oz/150 ml) dry
white wine
5 eggs, beaten
⅔ cup (3 oz/80 g) pecorino
cheese, grated
salt and pepper

Heat the oil and garlic in a large skillet (frying pan) over medium heat. Once the garlic has turned golden brown, add the meat and sear well over high heat until browned all over. Pour in the wine, season with salt and pepper, and cover. Reduce the heat and cook until all the liquid has evaporated.

Five minutes before the end of the cooking time, beat the eggs and cheese together in a bowl. Pour the mixture over the lamb, stirring constantly, and cook over low heat for a few minutes or until the egg mixture has thickened and formed a creamy film around the meat. Transfer to a warm serving dish and serve.

Note: If you find the flavor of lamb overpowering, soak the meat in a bowl of water with some vinegar for about 1 hour. Drain and pat dry before searing in hot oil.

Game

Game is popular in Italy and fairly readily available across the United States and UK. Nowadays, many game species, such as rabbit, deer, and boar, are raised the same way as well-cared for pigs and cattle, and buying farmed animals helps conserve wildlife in its natural habitat. It's also available all year around.

Leaner than most livestock, game lends itself beautifully to slow cooking and seasonal flavors, making for rich, unctuous wintry stews. Young game works well for roasting and frying, while older animals are better for stewing and braising. Classic recipes tend to pair game with fruit, either in the pan during cooking or served separately, as sauces. Chocolate and red meat have been being paired since the Aztecs first did so, and it's a combination that works particularly well with venison.

Pheasant, partridge, and quail are the chickens of the game world and can be found stocked in most good-quality supermarkets and grocery stores. They have less of a wild flavor than their free-roaming cousins but a more interesting flavor than chicken. If you can, buy ring-necked pheasant; it's a little more expensive but has a superior flavor. Once you've chosen your bird, it's time to decide: to hang or not to hang? Hanging is still popular in Europe, but less so in the United States; it ages and mellows meat, and many insist it's the only way to eat wild game. If you choose to, farmed pheasant should be hung for about a day in the refrigerator—a bird from a shoot needs three days—and a large cock pheasant is about enough for four people. Avoid dryness by laying pancetta or unsmoked bacon on the breast or slipping duck fat between the skin and the flesh. Partridge is lean, mild, and tender and doesn't need hanging unless it's been shot, in which case it'll need two to four days. A single small bird is enough for one person. Quail is probably the least gamey in flavor of all the birds; they're delicate with lean flesh and are normally cooked whole, partially boned. Technically a wild bird, all quail that you buy in stores will actually have been farmed, so if you want truly wild quail, you'll need to hunt it or find someone else who will. These plump birds are simple, versatile, and easy to cook, and take particularly well to marinating and stuffing.

Woodcock and snipe are similar-looking, migratory birds with characteristically long beaks. They are known as *beccacce* throughout Italy, but in the north they are also called *gallinazze*, *pizzacre*, or *pole* and in the south, *pizzarde* or *arcere*. They are not farmed and are found in Italy only at certain times of year— in October and November and in February and March. Different countries specify various hunting seasons. Both woodcock and snipe are pleasantly tasty and need hanging for three to five days. One woodcock or snipe is sufficient for two people.

These birds are great for roasting but they can dry out easily, so don't leave them unattended in the oven. They all also make superior-tasting broth (stock), which can be easily frozen for future use.

Most Italian venison comes from roe deer living in the Alps, but these are becoming increasingly rare in the wild and are now protected. In the United States, elk and moose are also classed as venison. It's a divisive meat in terms of flavor and can have a reputation for being tough, but if sourced and cooked properly, it can surpass all other meats. Depending on the diet of the deer, it can have the subtle taste of juniper or sage and varies dramatically depending on its age and how long it's been hung. They're lean animals and so are prone to drying out. What fat they do have, unlike pork or beef fat, doesn't taste pleasant, so it's important to keep this in mind. It's great for stews or braising—the saddle of a young deer is perfect for roasting, and the haunch and ribs are preferable for broiling (grilling) or frying. They can be used as a substitute for beef in many recipes and work well with whichever fruits or vegetables are in season, but they go particularly well with fall (autumnal) flavors, such as mushroom, turnip, and parsnip.

Most "wild" boar consumed in Italy is actually farmed, other than those from a few restricted areas in Tuscany and Lazio, where they still roam wild. It's a slightly different story in the United States, where they are present in 39 states, number in the millions, and can cause damage to crops and prey on smaller livestock. Humanely caught and slaughtered, they're a lean, sustainable meat resembling a darker, denser version of pork with a sweet, almost nutty taste. The cuts and cooking techniques correspond to those for pork (see pages 20–23). The loin, ribs, and legs of the young animal all work well for roasting and the ribs are great on a barbecue. Wild boar has become increasingly popular recently due to a renewed interest in healthy eating and slow cooking and a roasted boar shoulder makes for a great family feast.

Rabbit and jack rabbit (hare), similarly, have grown in popularity over the past few years. Both wild and farmed, rabbit in particular is widely available, but if you do buy farmed, try to ascertain its provenance from your butcher or meat supplier. The meat is white, lean, and tender and is best eaten when the animal is between three to twelve months old. The flavor is not dissimilar to chicken, but slightly sweeter and more gamey. It's usually roasted, baked in a pie, or braised in a stew to keep the meat moist. Rabbit is versatile, reasonably priced, and plentiful. American jack rabbit is equivalent to the European hare but much less highly regarded. Its unpopularity is largely due to its stigmatization as poverty food—and this is a huge shame. It's hard to come by unless you are a hunter, but if you can get your hands on it, it's well worth it. The meat is darker than rabbit, somewhere between duck and beef, and is gamey and delicious, perfect in stews with a lot of fresh herbs and root vegetables.

Coniglio ripieno alle olive

Rabbit Stuffed with Olives

Serves 4
Preparation: 20 minutes
Cooking: 55 minutes

1 rabbit, boned and with its liver
¾ cup (3 oz/80 g) pitted
    Cailletier olives
generous ¾ cup (1½ oz/40 g)
    fresh bread crumbs
½ cup (4 fl oz/120 ml) brandy
2 sprigs tarragon, chopped, plus
    extra to garnish
4–5 tablespoons extra virgin
    olive oil
2 cloves garlic
2 sprigs thyme
⅔ cup (5 fl oz/150 ml) white wine
salt

To serve:
Sautéed Jerusalem artichokes
    (page 264)
steamed new potatoes and
    trombetta zucchini (courgettes)

Photograph opposite

Preheat the oven to 325°F/160°C/Gas Mark 3. Lay the rabbit on a sheet of parchment paper.

Dice the rabbit liver. Roughly chop half the olives and mix with the bread crumbs, diced liver, brandy, and chopped tarragon in a bowl. Season with salt and stir in the remaining whole olives.

Cover the rabbit with the olive mixture. Use the parchment paper to roll the meat up from the shorter side, tie securely with kitchen twine, and rub with a pinch of salt.

Heat the oil in a large roasting pan, add the garlic cloves, thyme, and meat, and sear the meat on all sides. Pour in the wine and cook until it has evaporated. Transfer to the oven and cook for 45 minutes.

Cut the rabbit into slices, garnish with tarragon, and serve with the strained cooking juices, sautéed Jerusalem artichokes, steamed new potatoes, and trombetta zucchini (courgettes).

Note: The rabbit can be served cold, dressed with the hot cooking juices and accompanied by a simple beefsteak (beef) tomato salad.

Roasted Saddle of Rabbit with Artichokes

Serves 4
Preparation: 30 minutes
Cooking: 55 minutes

4 artichokes
juice of 1 lemon
2 saddles rabbit, cut into slices
4–5 tablespoons extra virgin
    olive oil
2 cloves garlic, smashed with
    the flat of a knife
2 oz/50 g prosciutto crudo, diced
⅔ cup (5 fl oz/150 ml) white wine
2 sprigs thyme, leaves only
salt and pepper

Photograph opposite

Preheat the oven to 325°F/160°C/Gas Mark 3. Peel the artichokes and trim the stems. Remove the outer leaves and trim the top. Cut in half. With a corer, scoop out and discard the fibrous choke. As soon as an artichoke has been prepared, drop it into cold water with some lemon juice. Bring a pan of salted water to a boil, drain the artichokes, and blanch in the salted boiling water for 5 minutes, then drain again.

Season the rabbit with a pinch of salt. Heat the oil in a roasting pan over high heat, add the rabbit and crushed garlic, and sear the meat for 5–6 minutes, or until browned on all sides. Add the diced prosciutto to the pan, then pour in the white wine. Let the wine evaporate gently, then transfer the pan to the oven and roast for 20 minutes. Add the artichokes and baste with the cooking juices. Cook for another 20 minutes.

Season the rabbit and artichokes with pepper, add the thyme leaves, remove the garlic, and serve.

Note: As an alternative, substitute the artichokes with 14 oz/400 g Jerusalem artichokes. Peel the Jerusalem artichokes, cut into slices about ¼ inch/5 mm thick, and blanch in a pan of boiling water for 3–4 minutes. Drain.

Coniglio al forno

Roasted Rabbit

Serves 6
Preparation: 10 minutes
Cooking: 1¼ hours

5 tablespoons olive oil
1 sprig rosemary
2 cloves garlic
1 rabbit, cut into pieces
salt and pepper

Preheat the oven to 350°F/180°C/Gas Mark 4. Heat the olive oil in a flameproof Dutch oven (casserole) with the rosemary and garlic, add the rabbit pieces, and cook, turning frequently, until browned all over. Season with salt and pepper, transfer the Dutch oven to the oven, and cook, stirring and turning occasionally, for 1 hour, or until tender. Transfer to a warm serving dish and serve.

Coniglio ripieno

Stuffed Rabbit

Serves 6
Preparation: 1¼ hours
Cooking: 1 hour 50 minutes

1 thick slice bread, crusts removed
1 rabbit, with liver
⅔ cup (3½ oz/100 g)
   chopped cooked, cured ham
7 oz/200 g Italian sausages,
   skinned and crumbled
¼ cup (2 oz/50 g) butter
1 tablespoon olive oil, plus extra
   for brushing
1 onion, chopped
1 sprig flat-leaf parsley, chopped
1 sprig thyme, chopped
1 egg, lightly beaten
1 clove garlic, finely chopped
1 carrot, chopped
1½ cups (12 fl oz/350 ml)
   dry white wine
salt and pepper

Preheat the oven to 400°F/200°C/Gas Mark 6. Tear the slice of bread into pieces, place in a bowl, add water to cover, and let soak for 10 minutes, then drain and squeeze out.

In a large bowl, combine the chopped ham and crumbled sausages.

Chop the rabbit liver. Heat half the butter and the olive oil in a pan, add the liver and onion, and cook over low heat, stirring occasionally, for 5 minutes. Remove the pan from the heat and stir in the soaked bread, then add the mixture to the bowl of ham and sausages, stir in the parsley, thyme, and egg, and season with salt and pepper.

Spoon the mixture into the cavity of the rabbit and sew up the opening with a trussing needle and thick white thread. Place the rabbit in a roasting pan, brush with olive oil, dot with the remaining butter, and sprinkle with the garlic and carrot. Roast until golden brown, then pour in the wine, cover with kitchen foil, and roast for another 1½ hours. Serve.

Coniglio in umido
Stewed Rabbit

Serves 6
Preparation: 20 minutes
Cooking: 1½ hours

3 tablespoons olive oil
1 rabbit, cut into pieces
1 clove garlic, chopped
1 sprig thyme, chopped
1 sprig flat-leaf parsley, chopped
¾ cup (6 fl oz/175 ml) dry
    white wine
2 tomatoes, peeled, seeded,
    and coarsely chopped
salt and pepper

Heat the olive oil in a large pan, add the rabbit pieces, and cook over medium heat, turning frequently, for 15 minutes, or until browned all over. Add the garlic, thyme, and parsley, mix well, and season with salt and pepper. Pour in the wine and cook until it has evaporated. Add the chopped tomatoes, reduce the heat, cover, and simmer, stirring occasionally, for 1¼ hours. Serve.

Coniglio alla cacciatora
Rabbit Cacciatore

Serves 6
Preparation: 30 minutes
Cooking: 1 hour 40 minutes

2 tablespoons butter
1 onion, chopped
2 oz/50 g prosciutto, chopped
1 rabbit, cut into pieces
¾ cup (6 fl oz/175 ml) dry
    white wine
1 sprig thyme
4 tomatoes, peeled, seeded, and
    coarsely chopped
pinch of all-purpose (plain) flour
    (optional)
salt and pepper
soft polenta (page 285),
    to serve

Melt the butter in a pan, add the onion and prosciutto, and cook over low heat for 5 minutes, stirring occasionally. Add the rabbit pieces, increase the heat to medium, and cook, turning frequently, until browned all over. Season with salt and pepper to taste, stir in the wine, and add the thyme, then cover and cook for 20 minutes. Add the chopped tomatoes, reduce the heat, and simmer for 1 hour. If the cooking juices are too runny, thicken them by stirring in a pinch of flour.

Transfer the stew to a warm serving dish, discarding the thyme, and serve with a soft polenta.

Coniglio all'ischitana

Ischia-style Rabbit

Serves 6
Preparation: 20 minutes, plus
   2 hours marinating
Cooking: 1 hour

3¼ lb/1.5 kg whole rabbit, cleaned
   and cut into pieces, liver and
   variety meat (offal) set aside
scant 1 cup (7 fl oz/200 ml)
   dry white wine
scant ½ cup (3½ fl oz/100 ml)
   olive oil
4 cloves garlic, unpeeled
large basil leaves, for wrapping
2 tablespoons lard
15 San Marzano tomatoes, diced
salt and pepper
herbs of your choice, to garnish

Photograph opposite

Put the rabbit pieces into a medium bowl, cover with the wine, and let marinate for about 2 hours in the refrigerator.

Heat the oil in a flameproof Dutch oven (casserole) over medium-high heat, add the unpeeled garlic cloves, and fry briefly until brown.

Drain the meat, reserving the marinade, and add to the Dutch oven. Sear the rabbit pieces well for 5–6 minutes, or until browned on all sides. Sprinkle with ⅔ cup (5 fl oz/150 ml) of the reserved marinade and let evaporate.

Wrap the liver pieces and variety meat (offal) in the basil leaves to make small packages. Add these to the Dutch oven with the rabbit, then add the lard and diced tomatoes, and season with salt and pepper. Cook over medium heat for 40 minutes, sprinkling with a little hot water if the stew starts to dry out. Season sparingly with salt and pepper.

Remove the stew from the heat, transfer to a warm serving dish, garnish with herbs of your choice, and serve.

Spezzatino alle noci

Rabbit Stew with Walnuts

Serves 6
Preparation: 45 minutes,
     plus 12 hours marinating
Cooking: 45 minutes

1 clove garlic, chopped
1 sprig thyme, chopped
1 sprig rosemary, chopped
3 juniper berries, lightly crushed
scant 1⅔ cups (13 fl oz/375 ml)
     dry white wine
1 tablespoon white wine vinegar
1 rabbit, cut into pieces
2 tablespoons butter
scant 1 cup (3½ oz/100 g) shelled
     walnuts, halved
5 tablespoons heavy (double)
     cream
salt and pepper

Put the garlic, thyme, rosemary, and juniper berries into a large dish, season with salt and pepper, and pour in the wine and vinegar. Add the rabbit and let marinate for 12 hours, turning occasionally. Drain the meat, reserving the marinade, and pat dry with paper towels.

Melt the butter in a pan, add the rabbit, and cook, turning frequently, until browned all over. Add about half the marinade and cook over high heat for 30 minutes, or until the liquid has almost completely evaporated.

Meanwhile, chop ½ cup (2 oz/50 g) of the walnuts and stir into the cream, then pour into the pan and cook until thickened. Transfer the rabbit to a warm serving dish. Stir the remaining walnuts into the sauce, spoon it over the rabbit, and serve.

Coniglio al miele con verdure

Rabbit with Honey and Vegetables

Serves 4
Preparation: 25 minutes
Cooking: 1¼ hours

6 tablespoons butter
1 tablespoon honey
1 rabbit, cut into pieces
5 tablespoons white wine vinegar
4 carrots, sliced
4 turnips, sliced
⅔ cup (3½ oz/100 g) peas
¾ cup (3½ oz/100 g) green
     (French) beans
1 sprig tarragon, chopped
salt and pepper

Preheat the oven to 400°F/200°C/Gas Mark 6. Heat the butter and honey in a flameproof Dutch oven (casserole), add the rabbit pieces, and cook over medium heat, turning frequently, until browned all over. Season with salt and pepper, remove from the Dutch oven, set aside, and keep warm.

Pour the vinegar into the Dutch oven and cook, scraping up any sediment from the bottom with a wooden spoon, then simmer over low heat until the liquid has evaporated.

Meanwhile, cook the vegetables in separate pans of salted, boiling water for 5 minutes, then drain. Return the rabbit to the Dutch oven, add the vegetables and tarragon, cover, transfer to the oven, and cook for about 45 minutes, or until tender.

Coniglio e patatine
Rabbit and Potatoes

Serves 6
Preparation: 15 minutes
Cooking: 35 minutes

2 tablespoons olive oil
2 tablespoons butter
2¼ lb/1 kg rabbit, diced
3½ oz/100 g flat pancetta,
    finely chopped
1 onion, finely chopped
all-purpose (plain) flour,
    for sprinkling
⅔ cup (5 fl oz/150 ml) dry
    white wine
scant ½ cup (3½ fl oz/100 ml)
    chicken broth (stock)
1 sprig parsley
1 sprig thyme
1 lb 2 oz/500 g (about 4)
    potatoes, peeled and diced
salt and pepper

Heat the oil and butter in a pressure cooker with the lid off over medium-high heat. Add the finely chopped pancetta and onion and sauté for about 5 minutes, or until colored. Add the meat and brown for 5 minutes. Sprinkle the meat with flour, pour in the wine and half the broth (stock), and let evaporate. Pour in the remaining broth, add the parsley and thyme, and season with salt and pepper. Put the lid on the pressure cooker and when you hear the first "whistle," reduce the heat to very low and cook for 20 minutes.

When the cooking time is up, open the pressure cooker carefully and add the diced potatoes. Replace the lid and cook for another 5 minutes. Remove from the heat and place the meat in a serving dish with the potatoes on the side. Serve.

Note: If you don't have a pressure cooker, cook the stew in a flameproof Dutch oven (casserole). Heat the oil and butter in the Dutch oven over medium-high heat. Add the meat and brown for 5 minutes. Do this in batches to avoid overcrowding the pan and then set aside. Add the finely chopped pancetta and onion to the pan and fry for about 5 minutes, or until slightly colored, then return the rabbit to the pan. Sprinkle with flour, add the diced potatoes, and pour in 2¼ cups (17 fl oz/500 ml) broth (stock). Add the parsley and thyme, and season with salt and pepper. Cover, bring to a boil, and simmer for 30 minutes. Serve.

Spezzatino al pomodoro e basilico

Rabbit Stew with Tomatoes and Basil

Serves 6
Preparation: 30 minutes
Cooking: 1½ hours

3 tablespoons olive oil
1 rabbit, cut into pieces
2¼ lb/1 kg tomatoes, peeled,
　seeded, and diced
1 onion, thinly sliced
1 clove garlic, crushed
10 basil leaves, chopped
salt and pepper

Heat the olive oil in a pan, add the rabbit pieces, and cook, turning frequently, until browned all over. Transfer to a plate, cover, and keep warm. Add the tomatoes and onion to the pan and cook, stirring occasionally, for 20 minutes. Return the rabbit to the pan, add the garlic, and season with salt and pepper. Cover and cook over low heat for 1 hour. Sprinkle the stew with the basil and serve.

Coniglio arrosto al rosmarino

Braised Rabbit with Rosemary

Serves 6
Preparation: 25 minutes
Cooking: 1½ hours

4 sprigs rosemary
1 rabbit
3 tablespoons olive oil
2 tablespoons butter
1 clove garlic
salt and pepper
Crunchy Roasted Potatoes
　(page 282), to serve

Photograph opposite

Chop one sprig of rosemary and set aside. Brush the rabbit with some of the olive oil and stuff with the remaining whole rosemary sprigs, half the butter, and the garlic, and season the cavity with a pinch of salt. Place in a pan with the remaining oil and butter, sprinkle with the chopped rosemary, and season with salt and pepper to taste. Cover and cook over low heat for 1½ hours, turning occasionally and adding a few tablespoons of hot water if the pan starts to dry out.

Remove the rabbit from the pan, cut into pieces, and place in a warm serving dish. Serve with crunchy roasted potatoes.

Bocconcini di coniglio allo speck con porri

Rabbit with Speck and Leeks

Serves 4
Preparation: 30 minutes
Cooking: 25 minutes

4 juniper berries
3 sprigs thyme, leaves only
1 rabbit, boned and cut into
   small pieces the size of a walnut
3½ oz/100 g speck dolce, in slices,
   cut in half lengthwise
4–5 tablespoons extra virgin
   olive oil
1 leek, trimmed and cut into thick
   slices on the bias
⅓ cup (2½ fl oz/75 ml) white wine
scant ½ cup (3½ fl oz/100 ml)
   vegetable broth (stock)
salt
Mashed Celery Root (page 265),
   to serve

Photograph opposite

In a mortar, crush the juniper berries with a pestle. Add the thyme leaves and pound with a pinch of salt. Cover the rabbit pieces with the pounded ingredients and wrap each piece in speck.

Heat the oil in a large pan, add the meat, and sear over high heat for 4–5 minutes, turning frequently, until browned all over. Add the slices of leek and season with salt. Pour in the wine and vegetable broth (stock), then cover, reduce the heat to low, and cook for another 20 minutes. Serve the rabbit with the mashed celery root.

Bocconcini di coniglio in agrodolce

Sweet-and-Sour Rabbit

Serves 6
Preparation: 40 minutes, plus
    2 hours salting and 6 hours
    marinating
Cooking: 45–55 minutes

3½ oz/100 g small carrots,
    cut into circles
3 scallions (spring onions),
    cut into circles
2 yellow and red bell peppers,
    cored, seeded, and chopped
7 oz/200 g asparagus, chopped
2⅔ cups (11 oz/300 g) fresh
    peas, shelled
3 tablespoons olive oil
1 x 2½ lb/1.2 kg rabbit, boned
    and meat diced
½ cup (4 fl oz/120 ml) wine vinegar
kosher or coarse salt, to sprinkle
salt and pepper

For the marinade:
⅔ cup (5 fl oz/150 ml) dry white
    wine
4 tablespoons olive oil
1 sprig rosemary
1 teaspoon superfine (caster) sugar
several black peppercorns
½ cup (4 fl oz/120 ml) balsamic
    vinegar

Photograph opposite

Put all the vegetables into a bowl, sprinkle with kosher or coarse salt, and let stand for 2 hours.

Heat the oil in a large skillet (frying pan), add the diced rabbit, and sear over high heat for 5–6 minutes, or until browned all over. Season with salt and pepper, reduce the heat to medium, and cook the meat for 30 minutes, sprinkling with hot water occasionally.

Bring a pan of water to a boil, add the wine vinegar, then add the vegetables and blanch for 3 minutes. Drain and place in a large heatproof bowl with the rabbit meat. Set aside and keep warm.

To prepare the marinade, bring all the marinating ingredients, except the balsamic vinegar, to a boil in a large pan with 2½ cups (20 fl oz/600 ml) water and cook until it has reduced by half. Add the balsamic vinegar, stir, and pour over the vegetables and rabbit. Marinate for about 6 hours before serving.

Note: Marinating the vegetables in salt part "cooks" them. This means that the subsequent cooking time in water is reduced.

Lepre con il ginepro

Jack Rabbit with Juniper Berries

Serves 6–8
Preparation: 45 minutes,
  plus 12 hours marinating
Cooking: 1¼–1½ hours

2¼ cups (17 fl oz/500 ml) dry
  white wine
10 juniper berries
1 bay leaf, torn into pieces
1 shallot, very finely chopped
1 clove garlic clove
1 onion, sliced
4 black peppercorns
1 jack rabbit (hare), cut into
  fairly large pieces
olive oil, for brushing
3½ oz/100 g pancetta, sliced
3 tablespoons brandy
2 tablespoons butter
salt

Combine the wine, juniper berries, bay leaf, shallot, garlic, onion, peppercorns, and a pinch of salt in a large dish. Add the pieces of jack rabbit (hare), cover, and let marinate for at least 12 hours in a cool place, turning occasionally.

Preheat the oven to 350°F/180°C/Gas Mark 4. Generously brush a roasting pan with olive oil. Drain the meat, reserving the marinade, and pat dry with paper towels. Wrap the slices of pancetta around the pieces of jack rabbit, place in the prepared roasting pan, and cook for 45–50 minutes, or until the jack rabbit is medium rare. If you prefer well-done meat, cook for an extra 15 minutes. Strain the marinade into a pan, bring to a boil over high heat, and cook until reduced by half.

Remove the roasting pan from the oven and unwrap the pieces of rabbit. Gently heat the brandy in a small pan, pour it over the meat, and ignite. When the flames have died down, transfer the jack rabbit to a warm serving dish.

Strain the reduced marinade into the cooking juices and bring to a boil over high heat, scraping up any sediment from the bottom of the roasting pan with a wooden spoon. Remove the pan from the heat, stir in the butter, and pour into a sauceboat.

Serve the jack rabbit with the sauce.

Lepre dolce forte

Sweet-and-Strong Jack Rabbit

Serves 6–8
Preparation: 30 minutes
Cooking: 2 hours 25 minutes

2 tablespoons olive oil
2 tablespoons butter
1½ oz/40 g pancetta, diced
1 jack rabbit (hare), cut into pieces
2 tablespoons all-purpose
  (plain) flour
¾ cup (6 fl oz/175 ml) red wine
¾ cup (6 fl oz/175 ml) meat
  broth (stock)
1 bay leaf
⅓ cup (2 oz/50 g) golden
  raisins (sultanas)
¼ cup (1 oz/25 g) pine nuts
2 tablespoons grated semisweet
  (plain) chocolate
1 teaspoon white wine vinegar
2 teaspoons superfine (caster)
  sugar
salt and pepper

Heat the oil and butter in a pan, add the pancetta and jack rabbit (hare), and cook over medium heat, turning and stirring frequently, until the pieces of rabbit are browned all over. Season with salt and pepper, sprinkle with half the flour, mix well, and cook for 10 minutes. Pour in the wine and broth (stock), add the bay leaf, reduce the heat, and simmer for 1½ hours.

Meanwhile, put the golden raisins (sultanas) into a bowl, add warm water to cover, and let soak for 15 minutes, then drain and squeeze out. Stir the raisins and pine nuts into the pan and simmer for another 30 minutes.

Combine the chocolate, vinegar, sugar, the remaining flour, and a pinch of salt in a bowl, then stir in 3–4 tablespoons water. Pour the mixture into the pan and bring just to a boil. Taste and add more salt if necessary.

Transfer the jack rabbit to a serving dish, cover with the chocolate sauce, and serve.

Lepre alla cacciatora

Jack Rabbit Cacciatore

Serves 6–8
Preparation: 30 minutes,
**   12 hours marinating**
Cooking: 2 hours 50 minutes

1 jack rabbit (hare), cut into pieces
white wine vinegar, for rinsing
2 sprigs thyme
2 sprigs marjoram
4 sage leaves
2 bay leaves
1 bottle (3 cups/25 fl oz/750 ml)
    full-bodied red wine
4 tablespoons olive oil
1 clove garlic
2 tablespoons tomato paste
    (purée)
salt and pepper
herbs of your choice, to garnish

Photograph opposite

Wash the pieces of jack rabbit (hare) in plenty of vinegar, then put the pieces into a bowl with a thyme sprig, a marjoram sprig, 2 sage leaves, and a bay leaf and pour in the wine. Cover and let marinate in the refrigerator, turning occasionally, for at least 12 hours.

Drain the meat, reserving the marinade, put into a pan, and cook over high heat, turning frequently, for 10 minutes, then season. Add the oil, garlic, and remaining herbs and cook, turning frequently, until the pieces of jack rabbit are browned all over. Strain the reserved marinade into the pan and bring to a boil, then reduce the heat, cover, and simmer for 2 hours. If the meat seems to be drying out during cooking, add a little warm water.

Mix the tomato paste (purée) with 2 tablespoons water, add to the pan, cover again, and simmer for another 30 minutes. Transfer to a warm serving dish, garnish with herbs of your choice, and serve.

Lepre alla moda di trento
Trento-Style Jack Rabbit

Serves 6
Preparation: 30 minutes, plus
   24 hours marinating
Cooking: 2 hours 10 minutes

1 x 3¼-lb/1.5-kg jack rabbit (hare)
all-purpose (plain) flour, to coat
bread crumbs, to coat
scant ¼ cup (2 oz/50 g) lard,
   finely chopped
1 small onion, finely chopped
2 tablespoons olive oil
broth (stock), for basting
salt and pepper
Polenta (page 285), to serve

For the meat marinade:
1 sprig rosemary
2 sage leaves
2 bay leaves
4 juniper berries
1 small onion, finely sliced
grated zest of ½ lemon
2 tablespoons red wine vinegar
4¼ cups (34 fl oz/1 liter) red wine

For the variety meats marinade:
4¼ cups (34 fl oz/1 liter) red wine
⅓ cup (2 oz/50 g) raisins
scant ½ cup (2 oz/50 g) pine nuts
grated zest of ½ lemon
pinch of ground cinnamon
2 cloves
1 teaspoon superfine (caster) sugar

Clean the jack rabbit (hare), removing and setting aside the liver, lungs, and heart. Cut the jack rabbit into pieces, rinse well, and pat dry. Put the pieces of jack rabbit into a bowl, add all the meat marinade ingredients, and season with salt and pepper. Cover with plastic wrap (clingfilm) and marinate in the refrigerator for 24 hours, turning the meat occasionally.

At the same time, clean and rinse the variety meats (offal), then coarsely chop into pieces and place in another bowl. Add all the variety meat marinade ingredients, cover with plastic wrap, and marinate in the refrigerator for 24 hours.

When ready to cook, remove the pieces of jack rabbit from the marinade and dry well with paper towels. Spread the flour out on a plate and place the bread crumbs on another. Roll the meat first in the flour and then in the bread crumbs to coat.

Put the chopped lard and onion into a large flameproof Dutch oven (casserole), add the oil, and cook for a few minutes over medium heat. Add the jack rabbit and cook until the meat is browned well on all sides. Add the chopped variety meat and its marinade, then baste with some broth (stock) and season with salt and pepper. Cover with the lid and cook over low heat for about 2 hours. If the Dutch oven starts to dry out, baste the meat with some hot water occasionally. When the jack rabbit and variety meat are cooked, the sauce should have a thick consistency. Serve with polenta on the side.

Note: Jack rabbit (hare) meat is very dry and rich because its water content is low. Extended cooking times, over medium–low heat, let it retain most of its nutrients and also require less baisting. The juices released from the meat during cooking are also high in nutrients.

Capriolo arrosto

Roasted Venison

Serves 6
Preparation: 35 minutes,
    plus overnight marinating
Cooking: 40–50 minutes

1 leg or haunch of venison
3½ oz/100 g pancetta, cut into
    thin strips
¾ cup (6 fl oz/175 ml) olive oil,
    plus extra for brushing
2¼ cups (17 fl oz/500 ml) dry
    white wine
1 sprig thyme, chopped
1 sprig summer savory, chopped
1 sprig oregano, chopped
salt and pepper

Make small incisions in the meat and insert the strips of pancetta. Combine the olive oil, wine, and herbs in a dish, season with salt and pepper, and add the meat. Cover and let marinate in the refrigerator overnight.

Preheat the oven to 425°F/220°C/Gas Mark 7. Generously brush a roasting pan with oil. Drain the leg of venison, reserving the marinade, place it in the roasting pan, and roast for 10 minutes. Pour the reserved marinade into the pan, reduce the oven temperature to 350°F/180°C/Gas Mark 4, and roast, basting frequently, for about 30 minutes. This will result in slightly rare venison. If you prefer it well done, roast for another 10 minutes, but do not overcook or it will become tough.

Remove the venison from the roasting pan, carve into slices, and place the slices in a warm serving dish. Spoon over the cooking juices and serve.

Capriolo in salmi

Venison Stew

Serves 8
Preparation: 45 minutes,
  plus 12 hours marinating
Cooking: 2½ hours

1 bottle (3 cups/25 fl oz/750 ml)
  red wine
2 pinches of freshly grated nutmeg
2 pinches of ground cinnamon
4 cloves
1 celery stalk, chopped
2 carrots, sliced
1 onion, chopped
1 clove garlic, chopped
4 sage leaves
2 bay leaves
4½ lb/2 kg stewing venison,
  cut into cubes
3 tablespoons olive oil
4 tablespoons butter
1 slice pancetta, diced
salt and pepper
herbs of your choice, to garnish

Photograph opposite

Combine the wine, half the spices, the celery, carrots, onion, garlic, sage, and bay leaves in a large dish, season with salt and pepper, and add the cubed venison. Let marinate for 12 hours in the refrigerator, stirring occasionally.

Remove the venison from the marinade and pat dry with paper towels. Strain the marinade into a bowl and reserve the liquid and the vegetables separately, but discard the cloves and bay leaves.

Heat the olive oil and butter in a pan, add the pancetta, and cook over medium head, stirring occasionally, until crisp. Add the venison and cook, stirring frequently, until browned all over. Add the remaining spices, season with salt to taste, and stir in the reserved vegetables. Cook, stirring occasionally, for 10 minutes, then pour in the reserved marinade and bring to a boil. Reduce the heat, cover, and simmer for 2 hours.

Transfer the meat to a warm serving dish and garnish with herbs of your choice. Transfer the cooking juices to a blender. Process to a purée, pour into a sauceboat, and serve with the venison.

Sella di capriolo arrosto ai mirtilli rossi

Roasted Saddle of Venison with Cranberries

Serves 6–8
Preparation: 25 minutes
Cooking: 2¼ hours

1 saddle of venison
4 tablespoons olive oil
4 tablespoons butter
2 carrots, chopped
1 onion, chopped
1 stalk celery, chopped
1 clove garlic
scant 1 cup (7 fl oz/200 ml) hot
    meat broth (stock)
scant ½ cup (3½ fl oz/100 ml)
    red wine
3 tablespoons superfine (caster)
    sugar
4 cups (14 oz/400 g) cranberries,
    thawed if frozen
2 tablespoons heavy (double)
    cream
salt and pepper

Photograph opposite

Preheat the oven to 350°F/180°C/Gas Mark 4. Gently rub the meat with salt and pepper. Heat the olive oil and half the butter in a large skillet (frying pan), add the venison, and cook, turning frequently, until browned all over. Transfer to a roasting pan, surround with the vegetables and garlic, and roast, basting frequently with the cooking juices and broth (stock), for 1½ hours.

Remove the venison from the roasting pan, carve into thin slices, place in a serving dish, and keep warm.

Remove and discard the garlic from the cooking juices, pour in the wine, and cook over high heat until reduced. Cut the remaining butter into small pieces, add to the roasting pan, and stir until the sauce is thick and velvety, then spoon it over the sliced venison.

Pour ¾ cup (6 fl oz/175 ml) water into a small bowl, add the sugar, and stir until dissolved. Pour into a pan, bring to a boil over high heat, and boil for a few minutes. Add the cranberries, reduce the heat to low, and simmer for 5 minutes. Stir in the cream and cook until the sauce has thickened.

Serve the venison with the warm cranberry sauce.

Cervo in agrodolce all'italiana

Sweet-and-Sour Venison Italian-Style

Preparation: 30 minutes, plus
   24 hours marinating
Cooking: 2 hours 20 minutes

3¼ lb/1.5 kg venison, diced
3 tablespoons olive oil
3½ oz/100 g pancetta, cut into
   thin strips
1 onion, thinly sliced
2½ tablespoons all-purpose
   (plain) flour
2 tablespoons raisins
2 squares bitter (plain) chocolate
3 tablespoons pine nuts, lightly
   toasted
salt and pepper
Polenta (page 285) or Creamy
   Mashed Potatoes (page 281),
   to serve

For the marinade:
1 bottle (3 cups/25 fl oz/750 ml)
   red wine
4 tablespoons red wine vinegar
4 tablespoons olive oil
3 cloves garlic
2 bay leaves
10 juniper berries
1 carrot
1 onion
1 stalk celery
1 sprig rosemary
1 sprig thyme, leaves only
2-4 sage leaves
black peppercorns

Put all the ingredients for the marinade into a bowl and add the diced venison. Cover with plastic wrap (clingfilm) and let marinate in the refrigerator for 24 hours.

When ready to cook the meat, preheat the oven to 300°F/150°C/ Gas Mark 3. Remove the meat from the marinade, then strain the marinade and set aside.

Heat 2 tablespoons of the oil in an ovenproof skillet (frying pan), add the pancetta, and sauté over medium heat for 1 minute, or until the fat has turned translucent. Remove the pancetta from the pan and set aside. Add the venison to the pan and cook for 10 minutes, until it is browned all over, then remove, set aside, and keep warm.

Using the same pan, add the onion and season lightly with salt. Sprinkle with the flour and when it has colored slightly, add the marinade and raisins. Stir until it is a thick sauce. Return the venison and pancetta to the pan and season with salt and pepper. Cover and cook in the oven for 1½ hours, sprinkling with hot water if the pan starts to dry out.

A few minutes before the end of the cooking time, add the squares of chocolate and let melt. Simmer until the sauce has thickened and turned shiny.

Transfer to a warm serving dish, sprinkle with the lightly toasted pine nuts, and serve with polenta or creamy mashed potatoes.

Cinghiale arrosto con composta di mirtilli rossi

Roasted Wild Boar with Cranberry Sauce

Serves 4
Preparation: 20 minutes
Cooking: 1 hour 55 minutes

3 tablespoons white wine vinegar
4 juniper berries
1 onion, sliced
1 carrot, diced
1 lb 8½ oz/700 g wild boar, cut
  into large chunks
1 cup (2 oz/50 g) fresh multigrain
  bread crumbs
3 tablespoons butter
1 tablespoon superfine (caster)
  sugar
grated zest and juice of 1 unwaxed
  orange
½ cup (4 oz/120 g) cranberry sauce
scant ½ cup (3½ fl oz/100 ml)
  red wine
salt and pepper
Creamy Mashed Potatoes
  (page 281) with thyme,
    to serve

Pour 2¼ cups (17 fl oz/500 ml) water into a flameproof Dutch oven (casserole) with the vinegar, a pinch of salt, the juniper berries, sliced onion, diced carrot, and chunks of wild boar. Bring to a boil over high heat and cover with the lid. Reduce the heat to low and cook for 1½ hours.

Preheat the oven to 400°F/200°C/Gas Mark 6 and line a roasting pan with baking parchment. Remove the meat from the Dutch oven and transfer to the prepared roasting pan.

Blend the bread crumbs with the butter, sugar, and grated orange zest in a food processor, then sprinkle the mixture over the meat and cook in the oven for 20 minutes.

Dilute the cranberry sauce with the orange juice, wine, and a grind of pepper in a bowl. Remove the meat from the roasting pan, cover with kitchen foil, and set aside.

Add the cranberry mixture to the roasting pan and heat over low heat for 5 minutes. Return the meat to the roasting pan and serve with the cranberry sauce and creamy mashed potatoes with thyme.

Note: If you want, a boned shoulder of wild boar can also be used for this recipe. In this case, the meat should be cooked whole in a pan for 2 hours and in the oven for 40 minutes.

Cinghiale in agrodolce
Sweet-and-Sour Wild Boar

Serves 6
Preparation: 20 minutes, plus
  12 hours marinating
Cooking: 1 hour 50 minutes

2½ lb/1.2 kg wild boar, cut into
  small chunks
5 tablespoons olive oil
1 onion, chopped
2 oz/50 g pancetta, diced
3 tablespoons puréed canned
  tomatoes (passata)
meat broth (stock), as needed
salt and pepper

For the marinade:
⅔ cup (5 fl oz/150 ml) red wine
½ cup (4 fl oz/120 ml) vinegar
½ onion, cut into thin slices
½ carrot, cut into circles
1 stalk celery, diced
1 sprig rosemary
sage leaves, to taste
parsley, to taste

Photograph opposite

Mix all the ingredients together for the marinade in a dish, add the wild boar, cover with plastic wrap (clingfilm), and marinate in the refrigerator for 12 hours, turning occasionally.

The next day, heat the oil in a heavy saucepan over medium-high heat, add the chopped onion and diced pancetta, and sauté for 5 minutes. Drain the meat, add to the saucepan, and cook until it is browned all over. Reduce the heat and pour some broth (stock) over the meat. Cover with the lid and cook for 1 hour 40 minutes, basting the meat with more broth if needed. Season with salt and pepper to taste, add the puréed canned tomatoes (passata) to the sauce, and let the ingredients heat through. Serve.

Bocconcini di cinghiale arrosto al vino rosso
Wild Boar Stew in Red Wine

Serves 4
Preparation: 15 minutes, plus
  24 hours marinating
Cooking: 3¼ hours

1¾ lb/800 g wild boar, cut into
  chunks
2¼ cups (17 fl oz/500 ml) red wine
4 juniper berries
3 tablespoons butter
3 oz/80 g slices (rashers) pancetta
2 leeks, trimmed and sliced
1 carrot, thickly sliced
salt
Puréed Lentils with Sage
  (page 285), to serve

Put the wild boar into a nonreactive bowl with the red wine and juniper berries, cover with plastic wrap (clingfilm), and marinate in the refrigerator for 24 hours.

When ready to cook, preheat the oven to 350°F/180°C/Gas Mark 4. Remove the meat from the marinade, strain the marinade, and set aside.

Melt the butter in a flameproof Dutch oven (casserole). Finely chop the pancetta and add to the Dutch oven with the meat and sear over high heat for about 10 minutes, or until browned on all sides. Add the vegetables and season with salt. Pour in the marinade and cook in the oven for about 3 hours, or until very tender. Serve with puréed lentils with sage.

Spiedini di filetto di cinghiale al mirto

Wild Boar Skewers with Myrtle

Serves 4
Preparation: 30 minutes, plus
    4 hours marinating
Cooking: 1 hour 10 minutes

1 lb 5 oz/600 g wild boar tenderloin
    (fillet), cut into chunks
4–5 sprigs myrtle
½ cup (4 fl oz/120 ml) myrtle
    liqueur
1¼-inch/3-cm stick cinnamon
4 cloves
2 tablespoons apple cider vinegar
3 tablespoons butter
6 pearl (baby) onions, cut into
    wedges
1 stalk celery, coarsely chopped
1 carrot, coarsely chopped
salt
cooked chestnuts, to serve
    (optional)

Put the meat into a nonreactive bowl and add the myrtle, myrtle liqueur, cinnamon, cloves, and vinegar. Cover with plastic wrap (clingfilm) and marinate in the refrigerator for 4 hours.

When ready to cook, put several wooden skewers into a bowl of cold water and let soak for 15 minutes and preheat the oven to 350°F/180°C/Gas Mark 4.

Remove the meat, strain the marinade, and set aside. Thread the boar onto the presoaked skewers and season with a pinch of salt. Melt the butter in a roasting pan, add the skewers, and sear on all sides until browned. Add the pearl (baby) onions, celery, and carrot, then pour in the marinade diluted with a ladleful of warm water. Cook in the oven for 1 hour.

Note: Make sure you cut the boar into equal-size chunks. This will ensure that the meat is cooked evenly within the specified cooking time. This dish can be served with chestnuts that have been boiled and sautéed in the cooking juices.

Cinghiale alle mele

Wild Boar with Apples

Serves 4
Preparation: 20 minutes
Cooking: 1¼ hours

4 tablespoons butter
2¼ lb/1 kb lean wild boar, diced
1 onion, finely chopped
1 carrot, finely chopped
1 tablespoon all-purpose (plain)
    flour
scant 1⅔ cups (13 fl oz/375 ml)
    red wine
1 clove garlic
1 bay leaf
4 tablespoons brandy
3 apples, peeled, cored, and sliced
salt and pepper
herbs of your choice, to garnish

Photograph opposite

Preheat the oven to 400°F/200°C/Gas Mark 6. Melt half the butter in a flameproof Dutch oven (casserole), add the meat, and cook, stirring frequently, for about 10 minutes, or until browned. Stir in the onion and carrot, sprinkle in the flour, and cook, stirring continuously, for 2–3 minutes, then gradually stir in the wine. Add the garlic and bay leaf, season with salt and pepper, and bring to a boil. Transfer the Dutch oven to the oven and cook for 1 hour, then stir in the brandy.

Meanwhile, melt the remaining butter in a pan, add the apple slices, and cook, stirring occasionally, for 10 minutes, or until golden.

Remove the Dutch oven from the oven and discard the garlic and bay leaf. Serve the meat in the cooking juices, garnished with herbs of your choice, and with the apple slices on the side.

Pernice farcita
Stuffed Partridge

Serves 4
Preparation: 35 minutes, plus
    10 minutes soaking
Cooking: 30 minutes

2 tablespoons butter, plus extra
    for greasing
1 thick slice bread, crusts removed
5 tablespoons milk
1 lb 2 oz/500 g mushrooms
2 partridges, plucked and drawn,
    with livers and hearts
3½ oz/100 g smoked pancetta
    diced
salt and pepper

Photograph opposite

Preheat the oven to 350°F/180°C/Gas Mark 4. Generously grease an ovenproof dish with butter. Tear the bread into pieces, put into a bowl, add the milk, and let soak for 10 minutes, then drain and squeeze out.

Separate the caps of half the mushroom from their stems and chop the stems with the livers and hearts. Put into a bowl, stir in the soaked bread, and season with salt and pepper to taste. Divide the mixture between the cavities of the partridges and sew up the openings with a trussing kneedle and thick white thread.

Chop the remaining mushrooms. Place the birds in the prepared dish, surround them with the chopped mushrooms and pancetta, and dot with the butter. Cover and roast for 20 minutes. Remove the lid, stir in the cooking juices, and roast for another 10 minutes, or until the partridges are cooked through and tender. Serve straight from the dish.

Fagiano arrosto ripieno
Stuffed Pot-Roasted Pheasant

Serves 4
Preparation: 40 minutes
Cooking: 45 minutes

1 pheasant, plucked and drawn,
    with liver
2 oz/50 g chopped smoked pork
    fat or thick-cut bacon
1 sprig flat-leaf parsley, chopped
1 small black truffle, chopped
    (optional)
2 oz/50 g pancetta, sliced
2 tablespoons butter
2 tablespoons heavy (double)
    cream
salt and pepper

Chop the liver, mix with the pork fat or bacon, parsley, and truffle, if using, in a bowl, and season with salt and pepper. Spoon the mixture into the cavity of the pheasant and sew up the opening with a trussing kneedle and thick white thread. Cover the breast of the bird with the pancetta slices, tie with kitchen twine, and season with salt and pepper.

Heat the butter in a large pan, add the pheasant, and cook over medium heat for 20 minutes. Remove the pancetta to let the meat brown and cook for another 10 minutes. Add the cream and cook for another 15 minutes. Return the pancetta to the pan and serve.

Note: If possible, choose a hen pheasant instead of a cock, because the meat will be more tender.

Fagiano alle olive

Pheasant with Olives

Serves 4
Preparation: 15 minutes
Cooking: 1 hour 40 minutes

1 pheasant, plucked and drawn
1 sprig rosemary
6 tablespoons butter
6 slices pancetta
5 tablespoons dry Marsala
2 cups (7 oz/200 g) pitted
   black olives
salt and pepper

Photograph opposite

Preheat the oven to 350°F/180°C/Gas Mark 4. Season the cavity of the pheasant with salt and pepper and put the rosemary and 2 tablespoons of the butter inside. Wrap the bird in the pancetta slices and truss with kitchen twine. Put into a flameproof Dutch oven (casserole), dot with the remaining butter, and roast, basting frequently with the Marsala and cooking juices, for 1 hour.

Remove the dish from the oven, sprinkle the olives around the bird, and cook over low heat for another 40 minutes. Carve and serve.

Fagiano al prosciutto crudo e porcini

Pheasant with Prosciutto Crudo and Porcini

Serves 4
Preparation: 25 minutes
Cooking: 50 minutes

1 pheasant, plucked and drawn
3 sprigs thyme, finely chopped
3 oz/80 g thin slices Tuscan
   prosciutto crudo
3 tablespoons butter
1 bay leaf
2 cloves garlic, smashed with
   the side of a knife
½ cup (4 fl oz/120 ml) white wine
1 lb 2 oz/500 g porcini, cleaned
   and sliced
salt and pepper
Mashed Potatoes and Cabbage
   (page 279), to serve

Preheat the oven to 400°F/200°C/Gas Mark 6. Season the pheasant inside and out. Rub the chopped thyme onto the pheasant breast and wrap in the prosciutto slices, overlapping slightly. Tie with kitchen twine and place in a roasting pan. Add the butter, bay leaf, and smashed garlic, and roast in the oven for 10 minutes. Pour in the white wine and reduce the oven temperature to 350°F/180°C/Gas Mark 4. Cook for another 20 minutes, basting the meat occasionally with the cooking juices. Add the mushrooms to the pan. Season with salt and pepper and mix with the cooking juices. Cook for another 20 minutes, or until the meat is ready.

Remove from the oven, cut off the kitchen twine, and remove and discard the garlic. Carve the pheasant and serve with the porcini, a splash of the cooking juices, and mashed potatoes and cabbage.

Fagiano arrosto con castagne

Roasted Pheasant with Chestnuts

Serves 4
Preparation: 20 minutes
Cooking: 1 hour

1 pheasant, plucked and drawn
3 tablespoons butter
2 slices (rashers) bacon, finely
    chopped
4 juniper berries, crushed
3 cloves garlic, smashed with
    the side of a knife
½ cup (4 fl oz/120 ml) brandy
7 oz/200 g chestnuts, boiled
1 bay leaf, cut into strips
salt and pepper
Puréed Brussels Sprouts
    (page 276), to serve

Photograph opposite

Preheat the oven to 400°F/200°C/Gas Mark 6. Season the pheasant inside and out.

Melt the butter in a flameproof Dutch oven (casserole) on the stove (hob). Add the pheasant, bacon, crushed juniper berries, and the garlic cloves, and sear over medium heat for 15 minutes, or until the bird is brown all over.

Transfer the Dutch oven to the oven and roast for 15 minutes. Pour in the brandy, reduce the oven temperature to 350°F/180°C/Gas Mark 4, and roast for another 15 minutes. Add the chestnuts, a pinch of salt, and the bay leaf, and cook for another 15 minutes, or until the meat is tender.

Remove the garlic cloves and serve the pheasant, cut into pieces, with the chestnuts, the cooking juices, and puréed brussels sprouts.

Spiedo di quaglie

Quails on the Spit

Serves 4
Preparation: 15 minutes
Cooking: 25 minutes

2 tablespoons butter, softened
2 teaspoons chopped rosemary
1 small onion, finely chopped
8 quails
16 slices pancetta
8 slices country-style (rustic)
    bread
olive oil, for brushing
salt and pepper
plain risotto, to serve

Preheat the oven to 350°F/180°C/Gas Mark 4. Combine the butter, rosemary, and onion in a bowl and season with salt and pepper. Divide the herb butter among the quails' cavities, then wrap each bird in two pancetta slices and truss with kitchen twine.

Thread the quails onto a spit, alternating with the bread slices. Brush with oil and set on a rack over a roasting pan. Roast in the oven for 25 minutes. Baste occasionally with the cooking juices. Serve with a plain risotto.

Quaglie al prosciutto crudo e zucchine

Quails with Prosciutto Crudo and Zucchini

Serves 4
Preparation: 30 minutes
Cooking: 55 minutes

4 quails
4 slices unsmoked prosciutto
    crudo
3 tablespoons butter
1 red onion, cut into quarters
⅓ cup (2½ fl oz/75 ml) white wine
12 baby zucchini (courgettes),
    cut into matchsticks
salt and pepper
sprigs rosemary, to decorate
    (optional)

Photograph opposite

Preheat the oven to 350°F/180°C/Gas Mark 4. Singe the quails to remove any remaining feathers. Season the inside and outside of each quail with salt and pepper. Cover the breast of each quail with a slice of prosciutto folded in half and tie with kitchen twine.

Melt the butter in a Dutch oven (casserole) over high heat, add the quails and onion, and sear the quails for 6–8 minutes, or until browned on both sides. Cook in the oven for 15 minutes. Pour the white wine around the meat, add the zucchini (courgettes) and a pinch of salt, and cook for another 30 minutes, basting occasionally with the cooking juices.

Remove the Dutch oven from the oven, cut off the kitchen twine and place the qauils on a warm serving dish. Arrange the zucchini around the birds, decorate with rosemary, if using, and serve.

Note: As an alternative, cut the zucchini into matchsticks, season with salt, and dust with flour. Heat enough oil for deep-frying in a deep fryer or deep skillet (frying pan) to 350°F/180°C, or until a cube of bread browns in 30 seconds. Deep-fry the zucchini for 4–5 minutes, then drain on paper towels and serve with the quails.

Woodcock with Juniper

Serves 4
Preparation: 20 minutes
Cooking: 35 minutes

12 juniper berries
7 tablespoons (3½ oz/100 g) butter
4 sprigs thyme
2 woodcock or snipe, drawn and
    plucked
¾ cup (6 fl oz/175 ml) gin
salt and pepper

Crush the juniper berries in a mortar with a pestle until mashed.
Blend one-third of the berries with 3 tablespoons of the butter and
shape the mixture into four balls. Put one butter ball and a sprig
of thyme in the cavity of each bird.

Heat the remaining butter in a large pan, add the birds, and cook
over high heat, turning frequently, until browned all over. Season
with salt and pepper and sprinkle with the remaining juniper berries.
Reduce the heat to medium and cook for about 25 minutes, or until
the birds are tender and cooked through.

Gently heat the gin in a small saucepan over low heat, pour it over
the birds, and ignite, then serve.

Beccaccia con mele verdi

Woodcock with Green Apples

Serves 4
Preparation: 15 minutes
Cooking: 25 minutes

2 woodcock or snipe, drawn
    and plucked
olive oil, for brushing
2 tablespoons butter
4 slices bread
2 green apples, peeled, cored,
    and cut into ¼-inch/5-mm
    thick slices
salt and pepper

Preheat the oven to 425°F/220°C/Gas Mark 7. Put the birds into
a roasting pan, brush with oil, and season with salt. Roast in the oven
for 10 minutes, or until golden brown, tender, and cooked through.

Melt half the butter in a large skillet (frying pan), add the slices of
bread, and cook until golden brown on both sides, then remove from
the skillet and set aside.

Heat the remaining butter in the same skillet, add the apple slices,
and cook until golden brown on both sides, then season with pepper.

Serve the birds on the slices of fried bread surrounded by the hot
apple slices.

Beccaccia al tartufo

Woodcock with Truffle

Serves 4
Preparation: 1½ hour
Cooking: 50 minutes

2 woodcock or snipe, drawn and
   plucked, with livers and hearts
80 g/3 oz pancetta slices
2 tablespoons butter
2 tablespoons olive oil
1 carrot, chopped
1 celery stalk, chopped
½ onion, chopped
1 bay leaf
1½ cups (12 fl oz/350 ml) red wine
2 small black truffles, shaved
8 slices Polenta (page 285),
   to serve
salt and pepper

Chop the livers and hearts and set aside. Tie the beaks of the birds between their legs, season the cavities with a pinch each of salt and pepper, and wrap them with the pancetta.

Heat the butter with the oil in a large pan, add the chopped carrot, celery, onion, and the bay leaf, and cook over low heat for 10 minutes, stirring occasionally. Add the birds to the pan and cook, turning frequently, until browned all over. Season with salt and pepper, pour in 1 cup (8 fl oz/250 ml) of the wine, and simmer over low heat for about 20 minutes. Remove the birds from the pan, cut them in half, and keep warm.

Add the chopped livers and hearts to the pan and mix well. Pour in the remaining wine, add half the truffle shavings, and cook until the sauce is slightly reduced.

Put the polenta slices in a warm serving dish and place the birds on top. Spoon the sauce over them and sprinkle with the remaining truffle shavings.

Poultry

Poultry is the term that's used to cover all types of birds that are raised domestically. Of these, chicken is the most popular in Italy. The standards of chicken farming are high there, unsurprisingly considering what store Italians set by quality in food, so it's best to follow suit when buying chicken for the recipes that follow—cage free or free range is good, but cage free (free range) organic is best—the meat will be more solid, less watery, and more flavorsome. The tendency in the United States is to use chicken as the most basic of meats, whereas Italian recipes, as you'll see, really focus on bringing out flavor. Where, in the United States, we might buy two chickens for larger gatherings or meals, Italians favor capon, which is available here. It's a castrated, fattened rooster. Where a large chicken will weigh 3–4 lb (1.4–1.8 kg), a capon can weigh as much as 8–10 lb (3.6–4.5 kg) and is full of flavor. In many parts of Italy, they're the traditional Christmas bird and are usually roasted whole.

Chicken broth (stock) is a very important part of Italian cuisine. Pasta and rice, most obviously risotto, is cooked *in brodo*, which means "in broth". If you have time, it's well worth the effort of making your own—it will always taste better than storebought. Few things are more satisfying than cooking something in broth you've made yourself, and it will make your home smell wonderful. Capon carcasses are particularly good for broth, but chicken and poussin also work well.

Poussin are younger chickens, 28 days or less, so they are smaller (14–16 oz/400–450 g), are usually cooked whole, and served one per person.

Geese are farmed mainly in the Lombardy and Veneto regions, where they're most popular, and they are usually eaten through the winter months when they're in season. The historic Jewish populations of Italy have had quite an influence—where Christian Italians have eaten pork, Jewish Italians have used goose in its place, making hams and sausages from it, which are popular to this day, as are goose ragùs. Geese are large birds, ranging from 10–14 lb (4.5–6.4 kg), but they are rich, so a large goose will feed a crowd.

Duck can either be farmed or wild but is seasonal in both cases, and is mostly eaten in winter in Italy. There is, however, variation: There are fat, mature birds with strong rich meat, which usually weigh about 7 lb (3.2 kg), and younger ducklings—smaller, more tender, and delicately flavored—which are rarer, but usually weigh 3½–4½ lb (1.6–2 kg).

Guinea fowl are a smaller bird, stronger than chicken in flavor, and slightly richer, but not fatty like goose or duck—less fatty, in fact than even chicken. They've been raised in Italy since the sixteenth century, and, unsurprisingly given that length of time, can be found in a great many Italian recipes.

Buying and cooking poultry

Always buy the best quality poultry you can afford—cage free (free range) and organic if you can find it—the results will be worth it.

Chicken

Make sure any chicken you buy is as fresh as possible. Young chicken roasts best. Cut away any lumps of fat and loose skin around the neck and cavity before roasting. Make sure you've taken out any bag of giblets from the cavity, and use it for making broth (stock). Dry the chicken thoroughly, inside and out, with paper towels before roasting, or the skin won't crisp. Salting the skin and the cavity will also help it to crisp. Remember to baste a chicken if you're roasting it. You can buy specific cuts (joints), or ask the butcher to cut up a bird for you. If you want to tackle it yourself, first remove the legs—cut down the side of the bird, from where they're attached to the body to the joint, then through the joint, between where the bones meet at the knuckle. Take off the wings in the same way. Then cut along the breastbone down to where you hit the rib cage, then, using the rib cage as a guide, slice down to the back of the bird and remove the breasts. Don't leave the oysters behind—they're in two semicircular depressions halfway up the spine, and are very tender little morsels. You can also cut up the legs by separating the thighs from the drumsticks at the joint. Use poultry shears to help you.

Duck

You can usually buy duck legs and breasts separately. If you're cooking a whole bird, you should truss it with kitchen twine so that it doesn't lose its shape—a lot of fat will come out. Follow the cooking directions in the following recipes carefully; overcooking duck will make it dry and grainy.

Goose

Geese are best bought in season and fresh instead of frozen. They can be large, so if you're intending to cook it in a conventional domestic oven, it would be best to buy one that's about 6½ lb (3 kg), which will be about eight to nine months old.

Geese are very fatty indeed, there will be large lumps of fat inside and sometimes on the underside of your goose—remove as much of it as you can before roasting. Always roast a goose on a rack in a deep roasting pan, and pour about ¾ cup (6 fl oz/175 ml) water into the pan before you begin so that fat won't smoke. So much fat will come off that you'll have to empty the pan a few times during roasting, adding another ¾ cup (6 fl oz/175 ml) water to the pan each time you empty it. Don't baste the goose or its skin won't crisp.

Guinea fowl

It's best to buy guinea fowl that are seven to ten months old—if a bird is older than that, it'll need to be a hung bird, which will taste far stronger. It should be cooked similarly to chicken—see the recipes for directions, but keep in mind that the breasts will dry out in the time it takes to cook the rest of it, so should be covered in pancetta or bacon to prevent that from happening.

Turkey

Native to the United States, turkeys have actually been farmed for a long time and, through selective breeding, they have developed from lean wild birds to fat domesticated ones. With current breeding techniques, males reach 31–33 lb/14–15 kg and females 15–18 lb/7–8 kg in five months. Among the females, the most delicious are the three month olds. Turkey is often stuffed. Classic stuffings include chestnuts, dried plums (prunes) and sausage, celery and carrot, and sausage and bread crumbs.

Before putting a turkey into the oven, brush it with oil or grease it with butter. Protect the breast with slices of pancetta or bacon. Place the turkey on one side for the first 45 minutes, then on the other, so that the breast does not come into contact with the roasting pan. Finally, place it on its back. Baste frequently while it is cooking. If there are not enough cooking juices, sprinkle with a little hot water. As soon as the skin turns golden brown, cover with kitchen foil. Cooking takes about 40 minutes per 2¼ lb/1 kg, at a temperature of 425°F/220°C/Gas Mark 7 for the first hour, and 350°F/180°C/Gas Mark 4 after that.

Cappone ripieno di castagne e datteri

Capon Stuffed with Chestnuts and Dates

Serves 6–8
Preparation: 30 minutes
Cooking time: 2 hours 35 minutes,
    plus 10 minutes resting

1 x 4½-lb/2-kg capon,
    excess fat removed
3½ oz/100 g bread, sliced
2 eggs
8½ oz/240 g) Parmesan cheese,
    grated (about 3 cups)
grated zest of 2 limes
pinch of grated nutmeg
7 oz/200 g chestnuts, boiled
    and cut into small pieces
8 dried dates, pitted and sliced
3 tablespoons butter
½ cup (4 fl oz/120 ml) white wine
scant 1 cup (7 fl oz/200 ml)
    vegetable broth (stock)
6 sweet, crunchy apples,
    preferably Anurka, rinsed
    and patted dry
salt and pepper
Puntarelle with Parmesan
    and Butter (page 256),
    to serve

Photograph opposite

Preheat the oven to 400°F/200°C/Gas Mark 6. Season the inside of the capon with a pinch of salt.

Break the bread slices into chunks and put into a food processor with the eggs, Parmesan cheese, most of the grated lemon zest, the nutmeg, and a generous grind of pepper, and blend all the ingredients together until smooth. Mix the chestnuts and dates with the bread mixture and use to stuff the capon. Sew up the open side with a trussing needle and thick while thread and tie the legs and wings together with kitchen twine.

Melt 2 tablespoons of the butter in a roasting pan and add the capon, breast side down. Pour the wine around the meat and roast in the oven for 30 minutes. Turn the capon over and reduce the oven temperature to 350°F/180°C/Gas Mark 4. Add the broth (stock) and cook for another 1½ hours.

Remove a long strip of the skin all the way around the circumference of the apples with a lime zester. Place a small curl of the remaining butter on each apple and arrange the apples around the capon. Cook for another 30–35 minutes, basting the meat with its juices.

Remove the roasting pan from the oven, sprinkle the remaining grated lime zest on top of the capon, and set aside for 10 minutes. Carve the capon and serve with the stuffing, apples, and puntarelle with parmesan and butter.

Note: Removing a long strip of the apple skin all the way around the circumference prevents the apples from splitting during cooking.

Pistachio and Pine Nut-Stuffed Capon with Fondue

Serves 12
Preparation: 1 hour
Cooking time: 1 hour 40 minutes

7 oz/200 g skinless, boneless
    uncooked chicken breast,
    chopped
5 tablespoons heavy (double)
    cream
3 egg yolks
scant 1 cup (2 oz/50 g) parsley,
    chopped
½ cup (¾ oz/20 g) thyme, chopped
¼ cup (1 oz/30 g) pistachios
¼ cup (1 oz/30 g) pine nuts
1 capon, boned and cut in half
    lengthwise (ask your butcher
    to do this if necessary)
pork caul fat
2 tablespoons olive oil
1 sprig sage
1 sprig rosemary
salt and pepper

For the fondue:
5 tablespoons butter
¼ cup (1 oz/30 g) all-purpose
    (plain) flour
2¼ cups (17 fl oz/500 ml) milk
pinch of grated nutmeg
scant 4¼ cups (1 lb 2 oz/500 g)
    diced fontina cheese
3 egg yolks
scant ½ cup (3½ fl oz/100 ml)
    heavy (double) cream
2 tablespoons Cognac

Preheat the oven to 350°F/180°F/Gas Mark 4. Blend the chicken, cream, and egg yolks together in a food processor until smooth. Transfer to a bowl, add the chopped parsley, thyme, pistachios, and pine nuts, then season with salt and pepper.

Season the 2 halves of the capon and cover with the mixture. Fold the 2 pieces in half and wrap in the caul fat. Tie with kitchen twine to form a cylindrical shape. Heat the oil in a large flameproof Dutch oven (casserole), add the meat, season with salt and pepper, and cook over high heat until browned all over. Remove from the heat, add the sage and rosemary, and cook in the oven for 1 hour.

Meanwhile, to prepare the fondue, melt the butter in a saucepan over medium heat. Stir in the flour and pour in the milk. Season with salt and pepper, add a pinch of nutmeg and the diced fontina cheese, and cook for 20 minutes stirring continuously. Remove from the heat, add the egg yolks and cream then return the pan to the stove (hob) and heat, without bringing it to a boil. Remove from the heat, add a splash of Cognac and stir.

Remove the capon from the oven, carve into slices, and serve with the stuffing and fondue.

Cappone farcito e salsa al marsala

Stuffed Capon with Marsala Sauce

Serves 12
Preparation: 1 hour
Cooking: 2 hours 20 minutes

olive oil, for oiling and drizzling
5 oz/150 g skinless, boneless
   uncooked chicken breast,
   chopped
1 egg yolk
scant ½ cup (1¾ fl oz/50 ml)
   heavy (double) cream
14 oz/400 g cooked ham,
   2 slices, diced
scant ¼ cup (2 oz/50 g)
   pistachios, diced
3½ oz/100 g sausage, diced
7 oz/200 g cooked chestnuts
   (about 20), crumbled
1 small black truffle, diced
1 capon, boned (ask your butcher
   to do this if necessary)
pat (knob) of butter
1 carrot, coarsely chopped
1 onion, coarsely chopped
2 stalks celery, coarsely chopped
2 cloves garlic, unpeeled
   and bashed
1⅔ cups (14 fl oz/400 ml)
   Marsala wine
salt and pepper

For the sauce:
2 sprigs rosemary, leaves only,
   chopped
1½ cups (12 fl oz/350 ml)
   Marsala wine
scant 1 cup (7 fl oz/200 ml)
   heavy (double) cream

Preheat the oven to 350°F/180°C/Gas Mark 4 and oil a roasting pan.

Blend the chicken, egg yolk, and cream together in a food processor until smooth. Mix in the diced ham, pistachios, sausage, crumbled chestnuts, and diced truffle. Season with salt and pepper and stuff the capon with the mixture. Sew the open cavity closed with a trussing needle and thick white thread and tie the legs and wings together with kitchen twine.

Place the capon in the prepared roasting pan and drizzle with a little oil. Add the butter, the chopped carrot, onion, and celery, and the whole garlic cloves. Cook in the oven for 1 hour, basting regularly.

After 1 hour, baste the capon with the Marsala and cook for another hour, basting regularly. Remove from the oven, take the capon out of the roasting pan, set aside, and keep warm.

To make the sauce, set the roasting pan on the heat, add the chopped rosemary to the cooking juices along with the Marsala, and let evaporate. Pour in the cream and cook until the sauce thickens. Remove from the heat and strain. Carve the capon into slices and serve with the sauce.

Pollo arrosto

Pot-Roast Chicken

Serves 4
Preparation: 25 minutes
Cooking: 1¼ hours

1 chicken
4 tablespoons olive oil
1 onion, chopped
1 carrot, chopped
1 stalk celery, chopped
1 sprig rosemary
salt and pepper
carrots in butter, to serve

Photograph opposite

Lightly season the cavity of the chicken and tie with kitchen twine. Heat the oil in a large flameproof Dutch oven (casserole), add the chopped onion, carrot, and celery, and the rosemary sprig, and cook over low heat, stirring occasionally, for 10 minutes. Place the chicken on top, increase the heat to high, and cook, turning occasionally, for 15 minutes. Season with salt, reduce the heat, cover, and cook for 40–50 minutes, or until tender and cooked through. If necessary, add a little hot water to prevent the meat from drying out.

Remove the chicken from the pan and remove the kitchen twine. Cut into pieces using poultry shears and serve with carrots in butter.

Galletti in crosta aromatica al timo

Poussin in a Thyme Crust

Serves 4
Preparation: 20 minutes, plus
**   30 minutes pastry resting**
Cooking: 45 minutes, plus
**   10 minutes resting**

4 poussins
4 shallots
2 unwaxed lemons, 1 cut into
    quarters, 1 sliced
all-purpose (plain) flour, for dusting
1 bunch parsley, leaves only
1 clove garlic, central core
    removed
salt
Brussels Sprouts with Pancetta
    (page 276), to serve

For the dough:
4½ cups (1 lb 2 oz/500 g)
    all-purpose (plain) flour
1 cup (2 oz/50 g) finely chopped
    thyme
7–8 tablespoons extra virgin
    olive oil

For the dough, mix together the flour with 1 cup (8 fl oz/250 ml) water, ⅔ cup (1 oz/30 g) of the thyme, 2 tablespoons of the oil, and a pinch of salt. Shape the dough into a ball, wrap in plastic wrap (clingfilm), and let rest for 30 minutes at room temperature.

Preheat the oven to 400°F/200°C/Gas Mark 6 and line a roasting pan with parchment paper.

Season the inside and outside of the poussins with salt and stuff each one with a shallot and a lemon quarter cut into segments.

Divide the dough into 4 equal portions. Roll out each portion on a lightly floured work surface to ⅛ inch/3–4 mm thick and wrap each poussin in it. Garnish each one with a slice of lemon. Transfer the poussins to the prepared roasting pan and cook in the oven for 45 minutes.

Wash and dry a handful of parsley leaves, and blend with a pinch of salt, the garlic clove, and remaining olive oil in a food processor or using a handheld blender. Let the poussins rest for 10 minutes, remove and discard their pastry crust, and spoon the remaining juices over each bird. Serve with the blended "pesto" sauce and Brussels sprouts with pancetta.

Pollo arrosto ripieno
Stuffed Chicken

Serves 4
Preparation: 50 minutes, plus
   10 minutes soaking
Cooking: 1 hour

4 bread slices, crusts removed
1 x 2¼-lb/1-kg chicken, with giblets
2 chicken livers, thawed if frozen,
   and chopped
3½ oz/100 g prosciutto, chopped
⅓ cup (1 oz/25 g) freshly grated
   Parmesan cheese
1 egg, lightly beaten
1 sprig rosemary
4 sage leaves
2 tablespoons butter
3 tablespoons olive oil
salt and pepper

Preheat the oven to 350°F/180°C/Gas Mark 4. Tear the bread into pieces, put into a bowl, add water to cover, and soak for 10 minutes, then drain and squeeze out. Season the cavity of the chicken.

Chop the giblets and combine with the chicken livers, prosciutto, soaked bread, and Parmesan cheese in a bowl. Season and stir in the beaten egg. Stuff the chicken with the mixture and sew the open cavity closed with a trussing needle and thick white thread. Tie the chicken with kitchen twine and tuck in the rosemary and sage.

Put the chicken into a roasting pan with the butter and oil and roast, basting frequently, for 1 hour, or until tender and cooked through. Insert a skewer or the tip of a sharp knife into the thickest part of the meat and if the juices run out clear, then it's done. Remove the chicken from the oven, cut off the kitchen twine, and cut into quarters. Take out and slice the stuffing. Place the chicken and stuffing in a warm serving dish and serve.

Pollo ripieno alla lucana
Basilicata-Style Stuffed Chicken

Serves 4
Preparation: 10 minutes
Cooking: 1¼ hours

pat (knob) of butter, plus extra
   for rubbing
5 chicken livers
2 eggs
3 tablespoons grated pecorino
   cheese
1 x 2¼-lb/1-kg whole chicken
few sprigs rosemary
few sprigs sage
salt and pepper

Preheat the oven to 350°F/180°C/Gas Mark 4. Melt the butter in a skillet (frying pan), add the chicken livers, season, and cook for 5 minutes. Remove from the heat and chop finely.

Beat the eggs with the grated pecorino cheese in a bowl. Season with a pinch of salt, then add the chicken livers and mix. Lightly season the inside of the whole chicken with salt, stuff with the liver mixture, and sew the open cavity closed with a trussing needle and thick white thread. Tie the chicken with kitchen twine and tuck in the rosemary and sage. Rub the chicken with butter and season.

Put the bird into a roasting pan and cook in the oven for 1 hour, or until cooked through, turning the meat and basting with the cooking juices occasionally. Insert a skewer or the tip of a sharp knife into the thickest part of the meat and if the juices run out clear, then it's done. Remove the chicken from the oven, cut off the kitchen twine, and cut into quarters. Take out and slice the stuffing. Place the chicken and stuffing in a warm serving dish and serve.

Gallina alla melagrana

Chicken with Pomegranate

Serves 4
Preparation: 20 minutes
Cooking: 1¼ hours

2 tablespoons olive oil
3 tablespoons butter
1 stewing (boiler) chicken
2 pearl (baby) onions
¾ oz/20 g dried mushrooms
4 pomegranates
1 cup (8 fl oz/250 ml) heavy
  (double) cream
4 sage leaves, chopped
salt and pepper

Photograph opposite

Preheat the oven to 350°F/180°C/Gas Mark 4. Heat half the oil and half the butter in a flameproof Dutch oven (casserole), add the chicken, and cook over high heat, turning frequently, until browned all over. Add one of the pearl (baby) onions and sprinkle with hot water. Transfer to the oven and roast for 1 hour.

Meanwhile, place the mushrooms in a bowl, add warm water to cover, and let soak for 15–30 minutes, then drain and squeeze out. Set aside.

Cut off and discard a slice from one end of a pomegranate, stand it upright, and cut downward through the skin at intervals. Bend back the segments and scrape the seeds into a bowl with your fingers. Repeat with the remaining pomegranates, then crush the seeds with a potato masher and pour the juice over the chicken. Return the Dutch oven to the oven. Reserve the pomegranate seeds.

Chop the remaining onion. Heat the remaining oil and butter in a skillet (frying pan), add the chopped onion, and cook over low heat, stirring occasionally, for 5 minutes. Add the mushrooms and cook, stirring occasionally, for another 15 minutes, then add to the Dutch oven.

When the bird is tender, remove it and the whole onion from the Dutch oven. Transfer the cooking juices to a food processor and process to a purée. Scrape the purée into a pan, stir in the cream and chopped sage, season, and cook over low heat until thickened.

Cut the chicken into pieces and slice the onion. Place the chicken in a warm serving dish and sprinkle with the reserved pomegranate seeds and sliced onion. Serve with the sauce on the side.

Chicken Stuffed with Mascarpone

Serves 4
Preparation: 50 minutes
Cooking: 30 minutes

3 tablespoons butter, plus extra
    for greasing
9 oz/250 g mushrooms
juice of 1 lemon, strained
1 clove garlic
1 tablespoon chopped flat-leaf
    parsley
4 skinless, boneless uncooked
    chicken breasts
2 cooked, cured ham slices, halved
scant ½ cup (3½ oz/100 g)
    mascarpone cheese
1 tomato
salt and pepper
mixed salad greens (leaves),
    to serve

Photograph opposite

Preheat the oven to 400°F/200°C/Gas Mark 6. Grease a roasting pan with butter.

Chop the mushrooms and sprinkle with the lemon juice to prevent discoloration. Melt 2 tablespoons of the butter in a small skillet (frying pan), add the garlic, and cook until it turns brown, then remove and discard it. Add the parsley and mushrooms and cook over high heat, stirring occasionally, for 5 minutes. Season with salt and pepper and cook for another 2 minutes, then remove the skillet from the heat.

Slice horizontally through each chicken breast without cutting all the way through. Open out each portion like a book, pound with a meat tenderizer, and season with salt and pepper. Place a piece of ham on one side of each piece of chicken, divide the mascarpone among the chicken breasts, and top each one with 1 tablespoon of the mushrooms. Fold the chicken breasts together again (like closing a book). Cut four slices out of the center of the tomato, place one slice on each chicken breast, season with salt, and dot with the remaining butter. Secure with toothpicks (cocktail sticks).

Place the chicken breasts in the prepared roasting pan, cover with kitchen foil, and roast in the oven for 15 minutes.

Meanwhile, preheat the broiler (grill). Discard the kitchen foil and brown the chicken breasts under the broiler.

Serve the stuffed chicken breasts with mixed salad greens (leaves).

Pollo alla cacciatora

Chicken Cacciatore

Serves 4
Preparation: 25 minutes
Cooking: 1 hour

1 chicken, cut into pieces
2 tablespoons butter
3 tablespoons olive oil
1 onion, chopped
6 tomatoes, peeled, seeded,
　and chopped
1 carrot, chopped
1 stalk celery, chopped
1 sprig flat-leaf parsley, chopped
salt and pepper

Photograph opposite

Put the chicken into a flameproof Dutch oven (casserole) with the butter, oil, and chopped onion and cook over medium heat, stirring and turning frequently, for about 15 minutes, or until browned. Add the chopped tomatoes, carrot, and celery, then pour in ⅔ cup (5 fl oz/ 150 ml) water, cover, and simmer for 45 minutes, or until the chicken is tender and cooked through. Sprinkle with the parsley, season with salt and pepper, and serve.

Note: This is the simplest way to prepare chicken cacciatore. In some regions, more celery and carrots are added; in others, white wine or broth (stock) is used instead of water; and in still others, sliced mushrooms are added.

Petto di pollo in fricassea

Chicken Breast Fricassée

Serves 6
Preparation: 10 minutes
Cooking: 30 minutes

1½ tablespoons butter
2 tablespoons olive oil
1 tablespoon all-purpose
　(plain) flour
1 sprig parsley, chopped
1 stalk celery, chopped
1 carrot, chopped
1 onion, chopped
1 cup (8 fl oz/250 ml) broth (stock)
2 skinless, boneless uncooked
　chicken breasts, diced
2 egg yolks
juice of 1 lemon
salt and pepper

Heat half the butter with the oil in a flameproof Dutch oven (casserole) over medium heat. Add the flour and stir. When it starts to brown, add the chopped parsley and chopped vegetables, and cook for 5 minutes. Pour in the broth (stock), then add the diced chicken. Season with salt and pepper, cover with the lid, and cook for 20 minutes, stirring occasionally.

Meanwhile, mix the egg yolks and lemon juice together in a bowl. Uncover the Dutch oven and pour in the egg and lemon mixture, stirring quickly so the sauce doesn't become too thick but is creamy and lightly coats the meat. Transfer to a warm serving dish and serve.

Spezzatino con acciughe e olive

Chicken Stew with Anchovies and Olives

Serves 6
Preparation: 20 minutes
Cooking: 40 minutes

scant ¼ cup (1¾ fl oz/50 ml)
    olive oil
1 x 2¼-lb/1-kg whole chicken,
    cut into medium chunks
4 salted anchovies
1 clove garlic, finely chopped
2¼ cups (17 fl oz/500 ml) puréed
    canned tomatoes (passata)
2½ cups (11 oz/300 g) pitted
    green olives
salt and pepper
chopped parsley, to serve

Heat the oil in a saucepan, add the chunks of chicken, and season with salt and pepper. Cook for 10 minutes, or until it is browned on all sides, then remove from the pan, set aside, and keep warm. Do this in batches, if necessary, so you don't overcrowd the pan.

Wash the anchovies under cold running water to remove the salt, then chop with the garlic. Add the chopped ingredients to the pan with the cooking juices, and sauté over gentle heat until the anchovies dissolve and the garlic is translucent, but not browned. Add the puréed canned tomatoes (passata) and bring to a boil. Add the chicken and the olives to the boiling tomato sauce, then add a few tablespoons of water until it just covers the meat. Return to a boil, then reduce the heat and simmer for about 25 minutes, or until the chicken is cooked through and the sauce has thickened. Remove from the heat and serve with plenty of chopped parsley.

Note: If you don't want such a strong olive flavor, you can reduce the amount of olives to 1½–2 cups (5–7 oz/150–200 g).

Pollo alla ligure

Ligurian-Style Chicken

Serves 4
Preparation: 15 minutes
Cooking: 40 minutes

3 tablespoons olive oil
1 x 2¼-lb/1-kg whole chicken,
    cut into pieces
⅔ cup (5 fl oz/150 ml) dry
    white wine
juice of 1 lemon
1 clove garlic, chopped
1 sprig parsley, chopped
1½ cups (5 oz/150 g) black olives
¼ cup (1 oz/30 g) pine nuts
salt and pepper

Photograph opposite

Heat the oil in a flameproof Dutch oven (casserole) over high heat. Add the chicken pieces, season with salt and pepper, and sear for about 10 minutes, or until browned all over. Pour in the wine and lemon juice and let evaporate. Add the garlic, parsley, olives, and pine nuts, then cover with the lid, reduce the heat to low, and cook for 25 minutes, or until the chicken is cooked through.

Uncover the Dutch oven and cook for another 5 minutes until the chicken is golden brown. Arrange the chicken pieces in a warm serving dish and serve.

Cosce di pollo con speck e olive

Chicken Thighs with Speck and Olives

Serves 4
Preparation: 20 minutes
Cooking: 30 minutes

olive oil, for oiling
6 chicken thighs, boned and
    skin removed
12 slices speck
1 shallot, diced
⅔ cup (5 fl oz/150 ml) dry
    white wine
1½ cups (5 oz/150 g) green olives,
    pitted and coarsely chopped
1 sprig marjoram, chopped
1 sprig parsley, chopped
grated zest of ½ lemon
salt and pepper
Creamy Mashed Potatoes
    (page 280), to serve

Preheat the oven to 400°F/200°C/Gas Mark 6 and oil a roasting pan with oil. Season the chicken with salt and pepper, then wrap the chicken thighs in the speck and add to the prepared roasting pan. Arrange the diced shallot between the chicken thighs, then place the roasting pan on the stove (hob) over high heat and cook for 5 minutes, or until the chicken is browned all over. Pour in the wine and cook in the oven for about 25 minutes, or until the thighs are cooked through. Add a little water if the roasting pan dries out. Insert a skewer or the tip of a sharp knife into the thickest part of the meat and if the juices run out clear, then it's done.

When the cooking time is finished, add the chopped olives to the roasting pan, remove the chicken thighs, and carve on a slant, then arrange the chicken slices in a warm serving dish. Cover with the cooking juices and olives, along with the chopped marjoram, parsley, and grated lemon zest. Serve with creamy mashed potatoes.

◆

Spezzatino di vino rosso

Chicken Braised in Red Wine

Serves 6
Preparation: 20 minutes
Cooking: 50 minutes

3 tablespoons olive oil
3 tablespoons butter
3½ oz/100 g pancetta, diced
1 x 3¼-lb/1.5-kg whole chicken,
    cut into pieces
10 pearl (baby) onions
½ clove garlic, crushed
7 oz/200 g mushrooms, halved
½ cup (4 fl oz/120 ml) grappa
1¼ cups (10 fl oz/300 ml) red wine
2 tablespoons all-purpose
    (plain) flour
salt and pepper

Heat the oil and 1 tablespoon butter in a saucepan, add the chicken, and cook for 5 minutes, browning each piece. Do this in batches, if necessary, to avoid overcrowding the pan, then add pancetta and cook for 5 minutes. Add the pearl (baby) onions, the crushed garlic, and the halved mushrooms. Season with salt and pepper. Add a splash of the grappa and carefully set it alight to flambé. When the flame has burned out, pour in the wine and ⅔ cup (5 fl oz/150 ml) water, and cook over medium–low heat for 30 minutes, or until the chicken is cooked through, turning the chicken pieces occasionally. Insert a skewer or the tip of a sharp knife into the thickest part of the meat and if the juices run out clear, then it's done. Place the chicken in a warm serving dish, cover, and keep warm.

Mix the flour and remaining butter in a bowl. Blend the cooking juices in a food processor or blender and pour into a small pan. Put over medium heat, add the butter and flour mixture, and cook until thickened. Pour the sauce over the chicken and serve.

Pollo profumato al Grand Marnier

Grand Marnier-Infused Chicken

Serves 4
Preparation: 15 minutes
Cooking: 1¼ hours

3 processed cheese slices,
   cut into pieces
2 oz/50 g pancetta, in 2 slices
   (rashers), chopped
2 tablespoons butter
3 sage leaves
1 x 2¼-lb/1-kg whole chicken
2 tablespoons olive oil
2 bay leaves
½ cup (4 fl oz/120 ml) white wine
½ cup (4 fl oz/120 ml) Grand
   Marnier
salt and pepper

Preheat the oven to 350°F/180°C/Gas Mark 4. Insert the cheese pieces, chopped pancetta, a pat (knob) of butter, and the sage into the cavity of the chicken. Season with salt and pepper.

Pour the oil into a roasting pan and add the remaining butter and the bay leaves. Put the chicken into the roasting pan and cook over high heat for 5 minutes, or until browned. Add the wine and let evaporate.

Transfer to the oven and cook for 30 minutes, then pour over the Grand Marnier. Cook for another 25 minutes, or until cooked through. Insert a skewer or the tip of a sharp knife into the thickest part of the meat and if the juices run out clear, then it's done.

Remove the chicken from the oven, carve into pieces of about the same size, and serve.

Spezzatino con i peperoni

Chicken and Pepper Stew

Serves 4
Preparation: 20 minutes,
   plus 1 hour marinating
Cooking: 50 minutes

2 large, fleshy yellow bell peppers
½ cup (4 fl oz/120 ml) dry
   white wine
3 cloves garlic, smashed with the
   side of a knife
scant ¼ cup (1¾ fl oz/50 ml)
   olive oil
1 x 2¼-lb/1-kg chicken, boned
   and meat diced
1 onion, chopped
1¼ cups (9 oz/250 g) canned
   chopped tomatoes
basil leaves, to taste
salt and pepper

Preheat the broiler (grill). Char the bell peppers under the broiler until they are blackened all over, then set aside until cool enough to handle. Remove and discard the skin from the bell peppers and cut the flesh into strips. Set aside.

Pour the wine into a small bowl, add the garlic cloves, and marinate for 1 hour.

Heat the oil in a skillet (frying pan) over high heat, add the diced chicken, and sear for 10 minutes, or until browned all over. Season with salt and pepper. Reduce the heat and cook for 20 minutes. Remove the chicken from the pan, set aside and keep warm.

Add the chopped onion to the pan with the cooking juices and cook for 5 minutes, or until colored. Add most of the wine and 2 of the marinated garlic cloves, and cook until the liquid is reduced by two-thirds. Add the chopped tomatoes, basil, salt and pepper, and cook for another 10 minutes. Return the chicken to the pan and add the remaining wine, the final garlic clove, and the peppers, and cook for 5 minutes. Serve.

Spezzatino di Gallina alla Vernaccia

Chicken Braised in Vernaccia

Serves 6
Preparation: 10 minutes
Cooking: 1¼ hours

scant ¼ cup (1¾ fl oz/50 ml)
    olive oil
1 whole stewing chicken,
    cut into 8 pieces
1 onion, finely chopped
1 bottle (25 fl oz/750 ml) white
    wine, preferably Vernaccia
⅔ cup (5 fl oz/150 ml) broth (stock)
finely chopped parsley, to sprinkle
12 slices toasted bread
salt and pepper

Heat the oil in a saucepan, add the chicken pieces, and cook for about 10 minutes, or until the meat is browned on all sides. Remove from the pan and set aside.

Add the chopped onion to the pan and gently sauté in the juices for about 5 minutes, or until translucent. Return the chicken to the pan, along with its resting juices, and pour in the wine together with a little broth (stock). Season with salt and pepper, cover, and cook over low heat for 1 hour, turning the chicken pieces occasionally.

Ten minutes before the cooking time is finished, sprinkle most of the chopped parsley over the meat. While still hot, arrange the stew over the toasted slices of bread, sprinkle with the remaining parsley, and serve.

Anatra al pepe verde

Duck with Green Peppercorns

Serves 6
Preparation: 3 hours
Cooking: 1 hour 40 minutes

3 tablespoons butter
1 onion, thinly sliced
1 carrot, sliced
1 stalk celery, sliced
1 sprig flat-leaf parsley
1 sprig thyme
1 x 4½-lb/2-kg duck
1 tablespoon green peppercorns
¾ cup (6 fl oz/175 ml) dry
    white wine
1½ cups (12 fl oz/350 ml) chicken
    broth (stock)
1 small red bell pepper, halved,
    seeded, and chopped
salt and pepper

Photograph opposite

Preheat the oven to 425°F/220°C/Gas Mark 7. Heat 2 tablespoons of the butter in a roasting pan, add the onion, and cook on the stove (hob) over low heat for 5 minutes, stirring occasionally. Add the carrot, celery, parsley, and thyme.

Rub the skin of the duck with salt and pepper, put the remaining butter, 3 of the peppercorns, and a pinch of salt inside the cavity, and truss with kitchen twine. Place in the roasting pan with the cooked vegetables. Cover the roasting pan with kitchen foil and roast in the oven for 15 minutes.

Remove the duck from the oven and reduce the oven temperature to 375°F/190°C/Gas Mark 5. Pour the wine over the duck and cook on the stove over medium heat, until the wine has evaporated. Add the broth (stock) and bring to a boil. Cover the pan and return to the oven for 45 minutes. Add more broth if the pan starts to dry out.

Keep the oven on, but remove the duck from the roasting pan. Strain the cooking juices into a bowl, stir in 5 tablespoons boiling water, pour back into the pan, and cook over medium heat until slightly reduced. Add the bell pepper and remaining peppercorns. Return the duck to the pan and roast in the oven for 15 minutes. Carve the duck, place in a warm serving dish, and spoon over the sauce.

Anatra arrosto con salsa di arancia e ribes

Roasted Duck with Orange and Red Currant Sauce

Serves 4
Preparation: 30 minutes
Cooking: 1 hour 40 minutes

1 x 3¼-lb/1.5-kg whole duck
4 unwaxed oranges
2 sprigs thyme
scant 1 cup (7 fl oz/200 ml)
    vegetable broth (stock)
8 sprigs red currant
½ cup (4 fl oz/120 ml) orange
    liqueur
1 tablespoon cane sugar
1 stalk celery, chopped
1 carrot, chopped
1 onion, chopped
salt and pepper
Sautéed Radicchio (page 254),
    to serve

Photograph opposite

Preheat the oven to 350°F/180°C/Gas Mark 4. Remove any excess fat from the duck and lightly season with salt and pepper. Insert the zest of half an orange into the cavity along with a sprig of thyme. Place the duck on a broiler (grill) rack inside a roasting pan so that it doesn't touch the bottom of the pan. Pour the broth (stock) into the pan and cook the duck in the oven for 1½ hours, basting occasionally with the cooking juices.

Peel 2 oranges, removing all the pith and skin, and cut out the segments over a bowl to collect the juice that is released. Squeeze the remaining oranges and remove the red currant berries from the stems. Set aside.

When the duck is cooked, remove it from the roasting pan and set aside in a warm place. Remove the broiler rack and skim some of the fat from the bottom of the pan. Add the orange juice, liqueur, sugar, a grind of pepper, the red currants, remaining thyme, chopped celery, carrot, and onion. Crush half the red currants with a fork and cook the sauce over medium heat for 10 minutes. Season with salt and strain the sauce.

Cut the duck into pieces, place in a warm serving dish, and serve with the sauce, orange segments, remaining red currants, and sautéed radicchio.

Anatra alla salsa di mandorle

Duck in Almond Sauce

Serves 6
Preparation: 30 minutes
Cooking: 1½ hours

4½-lb/2-kg duck, with liver
all-purpose (plain) flour, for dusting
2–3 tablespoons olive oil
1 onion
1 garlic clove
3 tomatoes, chopped
12 blanched almonds, roasted
5 tablespoons dry white wine
1 sprig fresh flat-leaf parsley,
　chopped
salt and pepper
potatoes mashed with freshly
　grated Parmesan cheese,
　to serve

Set the liver aside and cut the duck into pieces. Season with salt and pepper and dust with flour. Heat 2 tablespoons of the oil in a large pan over low heat, add the liver, and cook for a few minutes until browned on the outside but still pink in the middle. Remove from the pan and set aside.

Add the onion and garlic to the same pan and cook over medium heat, turning frequently, for 8–10 minutes, or until browned all over. Remove from the pan and set aside with the liver. If necessary, add 1 tablespoon oil to the pan, then add the duck and cook over high heat, turning frequently, until browned all over. Add the tomatoes, reduce the heat, cover, and cook.

Meanwhile, chop the almonds together with the liver, onion, and garlic. Put into a bowl, stir in the wine, and add the mixture to the duck. Add the parsley, season with salt, cover the pan, and simmer gently for an additional 1 hour, adding a little warm water, if necessary, to prevent it from drying out.

Place the pieces of duck in the middle of a warm serving dish, surround with two rings of potatoes mashed with Parmesan cheese, and serve.

Anatra alla birra
Duck Cooked in Beer

Serves 4
Preparation: 20 minutes
Cooking: 1½ hours

2 tablespoons butter
1 onion, thinly sliced
1 x 3¼-lb/1.5-kg duck
4¼ cups (34 fl oz/1 liter) beer
1 sprig rosemary
1 sprig thyme
2 sage leaves
1 tablespoon golden raisins
   (sultanas)
salt and pepper

Melt the butter in a deep pan, add the onion, and cook over low heat, stirring occasionally, for 5 minutes. Add the duck and cook over high heat, turning frequently, for 15 minutes, or until browned all over. Pour in the beer, bring to a boil, then reduce the heat to a simmer. Season with salt and pepper, add the rosemary, thyme, and sage, and simmer, basting and turning occasionally, for 1 hour, or until tender.

Meanwhile, place the golden raisins (sultanas) in a bowl, pour in lukewarm water to cover, and let soak for 30 minutes, then drain and squeeze out. Set aside.

Remove the duck from the pan and keep warm. Remove and discard the herbs and increase the heat to thicken the cooking juices. Stir in the raisins and simmer for a few minutes. Cut the duck into pieces, place in a warm serving dish, and spoon the sauce over them. Serve.

Anatra farcita al miele
Stuffed Duck with Honey

Serves 6
Preparation: 50 minutes
Cooking: 1½ hours

1 x 4½-lb/2-kg duck, with liver
2 tablespoons butter
3 tablespoons soy sauce
2 onions, chopped
½ clove garlic
5 tablespoons brandy
2 tablespoons honey
1 thick cooked, cured ham
   slice, chopped
salt

Preheat the oven to 350°F/180°C/Gas mark 4. Rub the inside and outside of the duck with salt.

Melt the butter in a skillet (frying pan), add the liver, and cook over low heat, turning frequently, for a few minutes, then remove from the skillet and chop.

Combine the soy sauce, onions, garlic, and brandy in a bowl. Transfer half the mixture to another bowl and stir in the honey. Rub the duck with the honey mixture, making sure it penetrates well. Stir 1½ cups (12 fl oz/350 ml) boiling water, the liver, and ham into the remaining onion-and-brandy mixture and stuff the duck with it. Truss the duck with kitchen twine. Place on a rack set over a roasting pan and pour a little water into the pan. Roast in the oven for 1½ hours, basting occasionally with the diluted honey mixture.

Remove the duck from the rack, remove the kitchen twine, and carve. Take out and slice the stuffing. Place the duck and stuffing in a warm serving dish and serve.

Filetti di anatra al fichi

Duck Fillets with Figs

Serves 4
Preparation: 30 minutes
Cooking: 1 hour 40 minutes

1 small duck, with liver
2 tablespoons butter, plus extra
    for greasing
4 fresh figs
1 cup (8 fl oz/250 ml) red wine
1 tablespoon lemon juice
½ white loaf, sliced and crusts
    removed
juice of 1 lemon
salt and pepper

Photograph opposite

Preheat the oven to 450°F/230°F/Gas Mark 8. Set the duck liver aside. Season the cavity of the duck with salt and pepper and truss with kitchen twine. Put the duck, breast side down, onto a rack in a roasting pan. Roast in the oven for 30 minutes, then turn over so the duck is breast side up. Reduce the oven temperature to 400°F/200°C/Gas Mark 6 and roast for another 1 hour.

Half an hour before the duck is done, cut the figs almost in half and open out slightly. Grease another roasting pan with butter, add the figs, and put a small piece of butter in each, then bake in the oven until lightly browned.

When the duck is done, remove the duck and figs from the oven. Cut off the wings, breast, and legs and break up the carcass with a meat tenderizer. Drain the fat from the roasting pan into a heatproof container. Stir the red wine into the roasting pan, add the carcass, and cook in the oven for 10 minutes. Remove from the oven but do not turn off the oven.

Pass the cooking juices through a food mill into a small saucepan and stir in the lemon juice. Chop the liver and add to the sauce.

Melt the remaining butter in a skillet (frying pan), add the slices of bread, and cook until golden brown on both sides.

Carve the duck legs into slices and cut the breast into fillets. Place the fried bread and duck in the middle of a warm serving dish, arrange the figs around them, and spoon the sauce over the duck.

Arrosto di oca con peperoni in agrodolce

Roasted Goose with Sweet-and-Sour Bell Peppers

Serves 8
Preparation: 3¼ hours
Cooking: 2 hours 20 minutes

1 x 6½-lb/3-kg goose
12 oz/350 g dried chestnuts
½ cup (4 fl oz/120 ml) olive oil
1 onion, chopped
1 carrot, chopped
1 stalk celery, chopped
1 sprig rosemary, chopped
¾ cup (6 fl oz/175 ml) white wine
4¼ cups (34 fl oz/1 liter) hot
  chicken broth (stock)
2 yellow bell peppers, halved,
  seeded, and cut into strips
2 red bell peppers, halved, seeded,
  and cut into strips
2 green bell peppers, halved,
  seeded, and cut into strips
2 tablespoons superfine (caster)
  sugar
¾ cup (6 fl oz/175 ml) white wine
  vinegar
salt and pepper

Photograph opposite

Season the cavity of the goose with salt and pepper, fill with the dried chestnuts, and truss with kitchen twine. Heat half the olive oil in a flameproof Dutch oven (casserole), add the goose, chopped onion, carrot, celery, and rosemary, and cook, turning the bird frequently, for about 20 minutes, or until well browned.

Meanwhile, preheat the oven to 350°F/180°C/Gas Mark 4. Pour the wine and 5 tablespoons of the hot broth (stock) into the Dutch oven, then transfer to the oven and roast for 2 hours, adding a ladleful of hot broth every 15 minutes and turning the goose every 30 minutes.

Heat the remaining oil in a large pan, add all the bell peppers, and cook over low heat, stirring occasionally, for 20 minutes. Stir in the sugar and vinegar and simmer gently for another 10 minutes.

Remove the goose from the oven and discard the chestnuts. Pass the cooking juices through a food mill. Carve the goose breast into slices, remove the legs and wings, and place in a warm serving dish. Surround with the sweet-and-sour bell peppers and serve with the cooking juices.

Oca arrosto con mele, albicocche e noci

Roasted Goose with Apples, Apricots, and Walnut

Serve 8
Preparation: 30 minutes, plus
   10 minutes soaking
Cooking: 2 hours 40 minutes

1 x 8¾-lb/4-kg goose, cleaned and
   any excess fat discarded
2 bay leaves
8 dried apricots
½ cup (4 fl oz/120 ml) Armagnac
1¼ cups (10 fl oz/300 ml) vegetable
   broth (stock)
8 walnuts
½ cup (1½ oz/40 g) rye bread
   crumbs
8 sweet, crunchy apples,
   preferably Anurka
1½ tablespoons butter
salt and pepper
Stewed Red Cabbage with Cumin
   (page 279), to serve

Photograph opposite

Preheat the oven to 375°F/190°C/Gas Mark 5. Rub the meat with a pinch of salt, then insert the bay leaves into the cavity and put the duck onto a broiler (grill) rack inside a roasting pan so that it doesn't touch the bottom of the pan. Pour the broth (stock) into the roasting pan and cook the goose in the oven for 2 hours, basting occasionally with the cooking juices.

Meanwhile, put the dried apricots into a bowl, add the Armagnac, and soak for 10 minutes. Coarsely chop the walnuts with the bread crumbs, then mix and season with a pinch of salt and a grind of pepper. Drain the apricots, chop coarsely, and add to the bread and walnut mixture. Core the apples with a corer, and while doing so, make a slightly wider cavity, and fill with the bread crumb mixture.

When the goose is cooked, remove from the pan, and carefully pour out any excess fat that has accumulated on the bottom. Arrange the stuffed apples around the outside of the pan and place a little curl of butter on top of each one. Put the goose back in the center of the roasting pan, without the rack, and cook for another 40 minutes. Serve the goose and stuffed apples with stewed red cabbage with cumin.

Stracotto d'oca

Goose Stew

Serves 8
Preparation: 3¼ hours
Cooking: 2¾ hours

1 x 6½-lb/3-kg goose
2 oz/50 g pancetta, thinly sliced
2 tablespoons olive oil
1 bottle (3 cups/25 fl oz/750 ml)
   dry white wine
1½ cups (12 fl oz/350 ml) white
   wine vinegar
4¼ cups (34 fl oz/1 liter) chicken
   broth (stock)
6 black peppercorns, lightly
   crushed
1 bay leaf
2 onions
pinch of chopped marjoram
pinch of chopped rosemary
1 lemon, sliced

For the sauce:
1 lemon
2 salted anchovies fillets, soaked
   in cold water for 10 minutes,
   drained, and chopped
2 tablespoons butter

Photograph opposite

Preheat the oven to 375°F/190°C/Gas Mark 5. Wrap the goose in the slices of pancetta, put onto a rack set over a roasting pan, and roast for 1½ hours.

Take the goose out of the oven and remove the pancetta. Place the goose in a snug-fitting pan with the olive oil. Pour in the wine, vinegar, and broth (stock) to cover. Add the peppercorns, bay leaf, onions, marjoram, and rosemary and season with salt. Simmer over low heat for 1 hour, then remove the goose from the pan, set aside, and keep warm.

To make the sauce, peel the lemon and remove any trace of bitter white pith. Dice the lemon flesh and add to the goose cooking juices along with the anchovies. Heat through gently, then remove the pan from the heat and stir in the butter.

Carve the goose into slices and place in a warm serving dish. Spoon the sauce over it and garnish with the lemon slices.

Oca ripiena di patate

Goose Stuffed with Potatoes

Serves 8
Preparation: 20 minutes
Cooking: 3¼ hours

4 potatoes, unpeeled
2 tablespoons butter
1 onion, chopped
1 sprig parsley, chopped
pinch of chopped rosemary
1 x 6½-lb/3-kg goose
1¼ cups (10 fl oz/300 ml)
   hot chicken broth (stock)
salt and pepper

Cook the potatoes in a pan of salted, boiling water for 10 minutes, then drain, peel, and dice.

Preheat the oven to 400°F/200°C/Gas Mark 6. Melt the butter in a pan, add the onion and parsley, and cook over low heat, for 5 minutes. Add the potatoes, increase the heat to medium, and cook, shaking the pan occasionally, until browned. Season with salt and pepper and stir in the rosemary.

Stuff the goose with the vegetable mixture, sew up the opening, and truss with kitchen twine. Prick the skin all over with a fork. Put the goose, breast side down, onto a rack set over a roasting pan, cover with a sheet of kitchen foil, and pour a little water into the pan underneath. Roast for 1 hour, then reduce the oven temperature to 350°F/180°C/Gas Mark 4 and roast for another 1 hour.

Remove and discard the foil, turn the goose over, return to the oven, and roast, basting occasionally with broth (stock), for another 1 hour. Skim off the fat from the cooking juices and pour them into a sauceboat. Carve the goose and serve with the cooking juices.

Oca brasata

Braised Goose

Serves 8
Preparation: 45 minutes
Cooking: 3½ hours

4 tablespoons butter
1 x 6½-lb/3-kg goose, cut into
   pieces
2 onions, thinly sliced
2 cloves garlic
1 bottle (3 cups/25 fl oz/750 ml)
   dry white wine
6 large tomatoes, peeled, seeded,
   and chopped
1 sprig rosemary
2 sage leaves
4 tablespoons brandy
salt and pepper

Preheat the oven to 300°F/150°C/Gas Mark 2. Melt the butter in a flameproof Dutch oven (casserole), add the goose, and cook over high heat, turning frequently, until browned all over. Add the onions and garlic, reduce the heat to low, and cook for 5 minutes, stirring occasionally. Pour in the wine, add the tomatoes and herbs, and season with salt and pepper. Cover, transfer to the oven, and cook for about 3 hours, or until the meat comes away from the bones.

Remove the goose from the Dutch oven, cut the meat off the bones, place in a serving dish, and keep warm. Remove and discard the garlic and herbs, then heat the cooking juices to reduce, if necessary. Pour in the brandy and mix well, season with salt and pepper to taste, and serve the goose with the sauce.

Spezzatino di faraona in agrodolce

Sweet-and-Sour Guinea Fowl Stew

Serves 4
Preparation: 20 minutes,
   plus 5 hours marinating
Cooking: 40 minutes

2¼ cups (17 fl oz/500 ml) red
   wine vinegar
2 bay leaves
2 cloves
10 juniper berries
1 x 2¼-lb/1-kg guinea fowl, cut
   into pieces
all-purpose (plain) flour, for dusting
4 tablespoons olive oil
3 tablespoons butter
2 shallots, chopped
⅓ cup (2 oz/50 g) raisins
¼ cup (1 oz/25 g) pine nuts
⅔ cup (5 fl oz/150 ml) Marsala wine
1 tablespoon superfine (caster)
   sugar
salt

Pour the vinegar and 1 cup (8 fl oz/250 ml) water into a large bowl, add the bay leaves, cloves, juniper berries, and a pinch of salt, then add the guinea fowl pieces, cover, and marinate in the refrigerator for 5 hours.

Remove the meat from the marinade, setting the marinade aside, and dust the meat with flour. Heat 1 tablespoon of the oil with half the butter in a saucepan, add the meat, and cook until browned all over. Do this in batches, if necessary, to avoid overcrowding the pan. Once all the pieces of meat are browned, set aside.

Heat the remaining oil and butter in another large pan over medium-low heat, add the shallots, and gently sauté until translucent. Add the guinea fowl and baste with a ladleful of the reserved marinade. Add scant ½ cup (3½ fl oz/100 ml) water and season with salt. Add the raisins and pine nuts, and cook over low heat for 20 minutes. Pour in the Marsala, sprinkle over the sugar, and cook for another 5 minutes, or until the guinea fowl is cooked. Serve.

Faraona ai carciofi

Guinea Fowl with Artichoke Hearts

Serves 6
Preparation: 45 minutes,
  plus cooling
Cooking: 1 hour 20 minutes

1 guinea fowl, boned
5 tablespoons olive oil
2 garlic cloves
5 globe artichoke hearts
1 sprig parsley, chopped
2 slices pancetta, chopped
2 tablespoons butter
1 sprig rosemary
5 tablespoons dry white wine
salt and pepper

Preheat the oven to 400°F/200°C/Gas Mark 6. Season the cavity of the guinea fowl with salt and pepper.

Heat 3 tablespoons of the oil with one of the garlic cloves in a pan, add the artichoke hearts, and cook until tender, then sprinkle with the parsley and season lightly with salt and pepper. Let cool, then put into the cavity of the guinea fowl, sew up the opening with a trussing needle and thick white thread. Tie with kitchen twine.

Put the bird into a roasting pan with the remaining oil, the pancetta, butter, remaining garlic, and the rosemary. Roast in the oven until the upper surface is browned, then turn over to brown the other side. Add the wine, reduce the oven temperature to 350°F/180°C/Gas Mark 4, and roast for about 1 hour, or until tender.

Remove the guinea fowl from the oven and untie the kitchen twine. Cut the bird into pieces and place in a warm serving dish with the artichoke hearts. Spoon over the cooking juices and serve.

Faraona al porto con uva e cipolline

Guinea Fowl in Port Wine with Grapes and Pearl Onions

Serves 4
Preparation: 20 minutes
Cooking: 35 minutes

1x 2¼ -lb/1-kg guinea fowl,
  cut into pieces
3 tablespoons butter
½ cup (4 fl oz/120 ml) white port
7 oz/200 g pearl (baby) onions,
  unpeeled
2 sprigs tarragon, chopped
1 bunch of pink grapes, halved
  and seeded
salt and pepper
Broccolini with Chile (page 272),
  to serve

Photograph opposite

Preheat the oven to 350°F/180°C/Gas Mark 4. Season the guinea fowl pieces with a pinch of salt and a grind of pepper. Melt the butter in a flameproof Dutch oven (casserole), add the guinea fowl pieces, skin side down, and sear for 10 minutes, turning the meat over so it browns on the other side. Pour in the port and let evaporate gently. Transfer the Dutch oven to the oven and roast for 20 minutes.

Meanwhile, bring a pan of salted water to a boil, add the pearl (baby) onions, and blanch for 10 minutes. Drain and add to the guinea fowl along with the chopped tarragon and grapes. Season with salt and pepper and cook for another 15 minutes before serving with broccolini with chile.

Faraona all'ortolana

Guinea Fowl Ortolana

Serves 4
Preparation: 30 minutes
Cooking: 1¼ hours

4 tablespoons butter
6 tablespoons olive oil
4 sage leaves
1 stalk celery, chopped
1 x 2¼-lb/1-kg guinea fowl,
    cut into pieces
¾ cup (6 fl oz/175 ml) white wine
8 pearl (baby) onions
3 potatoes, diced
2½ cups (11 oz/300 g) diced
    pumpkin flesh
salt and pepper

Photograph opposite

Heat half the butter and half the oil in a large pot with the sage, celery, and a pinch of salt and pepper. Add the guinea fowl pieces, and cook over high heat, turning frequently and occasionally adding the wine, for about 10 minutes, or until browned all over.

Heat the remaining butter and oil in another pan, add the pearl (baby) onions, diced potatoes, and pumpkin, season with salt and pepper, and cook over low heat for 40 minutes, stirring occasionally.

Preheat the oven to 350°F/180°C/Gas Mark 4. Transfer the vegetables, herbs, and guinea fowl to a roasting pan and roast in the oven for 30 minutes, or until cooked through. Serve.

Faraona con crema alle erbe

Guinea Fowl in a Herb Sauce

Serves 4
Preparation: 25 minutes
Cooking: 1 hour 20 minutes

3 tablespoons olive oil
2 tablespoons butter, plus
    a pat (knob)
1 x 2¼-lb/1-kg guinea fowl,
    cut into quarters
⅔ cup (5 fl oz/150 ml) broth
    (stock)
⅔ cup (5 fl oz/150 ml) white wine
1 onion, sliced
1 sprig parsley
1 sprig basil
pinch of thyme
2 bay leaves
8 green peppercorns
½ cup (1½ oz/40 g) finely
    grated pecorino
salt

Heat the oil and 2 tablespoons butter in a large saucepan. Add the guinea fowl quarters, season with salt, then add the broth (stock) followed by the wine. Add the onion with the parsley, basil, thyme, bay leaves, and green peppercorns. Cover with a lid and cook over medium-low heat for 1 hour. Remove the guinea fowl, cover, and keep warm.

Preheat the oven to 400°F/200°C/Gas Mark 6. Add the pat (knob) of butter to the cooking juices in the pan and stir to combine. Pour half of this sauce into a large ovenproof dish and sprinkle with half of the finely grated pecorino. Add the guinea fowl and the remaining sauce and pecorino, cover with foil, and cook in the oven for 15 minutes. Remove from the oven and serve.

Faraona speziata allo yogurt

Spiced Guinea Fowl with Yogurt

Serves 4
Preparation: 20 minutes
Cooking: 45 minutes

2 green cardamom pods
½ teaspoon coriander seeds
4 tablespoons extra virgin olive oil
1 x 1¼-inch/3-cm stick cinnamon
1 x 2¼-lb/1-kg guinea fowl, cut
   into pieces
½ cup (4 fl oz/120 ml) white wine
4 scallions (spring onions), trimmed
   and cut into rings
1 cup (8 fl oz/250 ml) plain yogurt
⅔ cup (¾ oz/20 g) fresh cilantro
   (coriander), chopped
salt and pepper
Mashed Potatoes with Lime
   (page 282), to serve

Photograph opposite

Preheat the oven to 350°F/180°C/Gas Mark 4. Crush the cardamom pods in a mortar using a pestle and remove the seeds. Crush these seeds in a mortar with the coriander seeds to a fine powder.

Heat the olive oil in a flameproof Dutch oven (casserole), add the spices and cinnamon stick, and roast for a few seconds. Add the guinea fowl pieces and sear on all sides until browned all over. Pour in the wine and let evaporate gently. Add the scallions (spring onions) to the Dutch oven, season with salt and pepper, and cook in the oven for 30 minutes.

Remove the cinnamon stick and place the guinea fowl pieces in a warm serving dish. Add the yogurt to the cooking juices and stir over the heat for 2 minutes. Cover the guinea fowl with the sauce, sprinkle with chopped cilantro (coriander), and serve with mashed potatoes with lime.

Spezzatino al rosmarino e marsala

Guinea Fowl Stew with Rosemary and Marsala

Serves 12
Preparation: 45 minutes
Cooking: 1 hour 20 minutes

1¼ sticks (5 oz/150 g) butter
3 carrots, chopped
3 stalks celery, chopped
2 sprigs rosemary, leaves chopped
3 cloves garlic
4 juniper berries
3 x 2¼-lb/1-kg guinea fowl, cut
   into chunks, bones set aside
2½ cups (20 fl oz/600 ml)
   Marsala wine
⅔ cup (5 fl oz/150 ml) heavy
   (double) cream
salt and pepper

Melt the butter in a large saucepan over medium-low heat, add the chopped carrots, celery, and rosemary, the whole garlic cloves, and juniper berries, and cook for 10 minutes. Add the guinea fowl and the bones and cook until the meat colors. Season with salt and pepper, then cover with a lid and cook for 30 minutes. Pour in the Marsala and cook for another 30 minutes.

Remove the pan from the heat and, using a slotted spoon, take the meat and bones out of the pan. Set the meat aside and keep warm. Discard the bones.

Pour the cream into the cooking juices in the pan and bring to a boil. Boil for about 5 minutes, then pour into a blender and blend until smooth. Serve the guinea fowl with the still warm sauce.

Arrosto di faraona
Pot-Roast Guinea Fowl

Serves 6
Preparation: 30 minutes
Cooking: 1¼ hours

1 x 2¼-lb/1-kg guinea fowl
1 sprig rosemary
2 sage leaves
2 oz/50 g pancetta slices
3 tablespoons butter
3 tablespoons olive oil
¾ cup (6 fl oz/175 ml) dry
   white wine
salt and pepper

Photograph opposite

Season the cavity of the guinea fowl with salt and pepper and put the rosemary, sage, one of the pancetta slices, and 1 tablespoon of the butter into the cavity. Cover the breast of the bird with the remaining pancetta slices and tie with kitchen twine. Season with salt and pepper.

Heat the remaining butter and the oil in a large pan, add the guinea fowl, and cook, turning frequently, until browned all over. Pour in half the wine and cook until it has evaporated, then cover and cook over low heat for 50 minutes. Remove the pancetta slices and set aside. Cover the pan and cook for another 10 minutes. Remove the guinea fowl from the pan, set aside, and keep warm.

Stir the remaining wine into the pan and cook until reduced by half. Cut the guinea fowl into pieces, place in a warm serving dish with the pancetta slices, spoon over the cooking juices, and serve.

Arrosto di tacchinella
Pot-Roast Turkey

Serves 8
Preparation: 25 minutes
Cooking: 1¾–2 hours

1 x 6½-lb/3-kg turkey
2 sprigs rosemary
4 sage leaves
2 slices prosciutto, cut into strips
3½ oz/100 g pancetta, sliced
3 tablespoons olive oil
2 tablespoons butter
2 tablespoons grappa
salt and pepper

Season the cavity of the turkey with salt and pepper and put one of the rosemary sprigs, the sage, and prosciutto into the cavity. Sew up the opening with a trussing needle and thick white thread, wrap the turkey breast with pancetta, and truss with kitchen twine.

Put the oil, butter, and remaining rosemary into a large, shallow pan, add the turkey, and cook over low heat, turning and basting occasionally, for 1¾–2 hours, or until tender and cooked through. Season lightly with salt once or twice during cooking.

About 10 minutes before the end of the cooking time, remove the pancetta to let the turkey brown completely. Sprinkle with the grappa and ignite. Serve when the flames have died down.

Arrosto di tacchino con pomodorini e basilico

Roasted Turkey with Cherry Tomatoes and Basil

Serves 4
Preparation: 20 minutes
Cooking: 50 minutes

1¾ lb/800 g boneless turkey breast
1 clove garlic, cut into thin
    matchsticks
5–6 tablespoons extra virgin
    olive oil
1¾ cups (11 oz/300 g) cherry
    tomatoes, stems removed
½ cup (4 fl oz/120 ml) white wine
⅓ cup (1½ oz/40 g) pine nuts, plus
    extra to garnish
generous handful of basil leaves,
    washed and patted dry
salt
Grilled Violet Eggplants
    (page 266), to serve

Photograph opposite

Preheat the oven to 350°F/180°C/Gas Mark 4. Using a sharp knife, make several incisions in the turkey breast and insert the garlic sticks into each cut. Season the meat with salt and tie securely with kitchen twine.

Heat the olive oil in a roasting pan over high heat, add the meat, and sear, turning on all sides, until brown. Using the tip of a knife, make a small incision in the tomatoes and add to the meat. Pour in the wine and season with salt. Cook in the oven for 30 minutes, then add the pine nuts and cook for another 15 minutes. Remove the turkey from the roasting pan, set aside and keep warm.

Put the basil (reserving a few leaves to garnish) into a food processor with the cooking juices, pine nuts, and half the tomatoes. Blend well.

Remove the kitchen twine and carve the meat into slices. Place on a serving dish with the remaining whole tomatoes and grilled violet eggplants and cover with the sauce. Sprinkle with pine nuts and the reserved basil leaves and serve.

Tacchino ripieno di castagne

Turkey Stuffed with Chestnuts

Serves 6–8
Preparation: 1½ hours
Cooking: 2 hours

9 oz/250 g shelled chestnuts,
    boiled for about 45 minutes
11 oz/300 g Italian sausages,
    skinned and crumbled
1¼ cups (5 oz/150 g) chopped
    pitted green olives
1 x 6½-lb-3-kg turkey
3½ oz/100 g pancetta, sliced
olive oil, for brushing
salt and pepper
lettuce leaves, to serve

Peel off the skins and mash the chestnuts. Preheat the oven to 350°F/180°C/Gas Mark 4. Add the sausages and olives to the chestnuts, season with salt and pepper, and mix well. Spoon the mixture into the cavity of the turkey and sew up the opening. Cover the turkey breast with the pancetta slices, tie with kitchen twine, and season with salt and pepper.

Generously brush a roasting pan with oil, put the turkey into it, and roast in the oven, basting occasionally, for 1½ hours. Remove the pancetta slices, return the turkey to the oven, and roast for another 30 minutes, or until browned, cooked through, and tender.

Place the turkey in a warm serving dish, carve into slices, and serve with the pancetta slices, chestnut stuffing, and large lettuce leaves.

Fricassea ai porcini
Turkey Fricassée with Porcini

Serves 4
Preparation: 25 minutes
Cooking: 1¼ hours

3 tablespoons butter
3 tablespoons olive oil
1 lb 5 oz/600 g skinless,
   boneless turkey breast,
   cut into medium cubes
1 small onion, chopped
2 cloves garlic
¾ cup (6 fl oz/175 ml) dry
   white wine
14 oz/400 g porcini, sliced
1 sprig flat-leaf parsley, chopped
5 tablespoons hot chicken or
   turkey broth (stock) made
   with a bouillon (stock) cube
2 egg yolks
juice of ½ lemon, strained
salt and pepper

Photograph opposite

Heat the butter and 2 tablespoons of the olive oil in a large pan, add the turkey, and cook over high heat, stirring frequently, until golden brown. Remove with a slotted spoon and set aside.

Reduce the heat, add the onion and 1 garlic clove to the pan, and cook, stirring occasionally, for 5 minutes, then remove and discard the garlic. Return the turkey to the pan, pour in the wine, cover, and simmer for 30 minutes. Brush the porcini with the remaining olive oil and stir into the pan. Chop the remaining garlic clove and add to the pan with the parsley. Pour in the hot broth (stock) and simmer for another 30 minutes.

Beat the egg yolks with 1 tablespoon water, the lemon juice, a pinch of salt, and a pinch of pepper in a bowl. Move the pan to the edge of the stove (hob), pour in the egg mixture, and mix quickly so that it does not curdle but remains soft and creamy and coats the meat lightly. Transfer to a warm serving dish and serve.

Tacchino ripieno di cavolini di bruxelles
Turkey Stuffed with Brussels Sprouts

Serves 6–8
Preparation: 1 hour
Cooking: 2¼ hours, plus
   10 minutes resting

11 oz/300 g Brussels sprouts,
   trimmed
1¾ cups (9 oz/250 g) chopped
   cooked, cured ham
1 x 6½-lb/3-kg turkey
3½ oz/100 g pork fat, thinly
   sliced, or thick-cut bacon
   slices (rashers)
olive oil, for brushing
salt and pepper

Preheat the oven to 350°F/180°C/Gas Mark 4. Cook the Brussels sprouts in a large pan of salted, boiling water, for about 15 minutes, or until tender, then drain and halve. Put them into a bowl, add the ham, season with salt and pepper, and mix well. Spoon the mixture into the cavity of the turkey and sew up the opening with a trussing needle and thick white thread. Cover the turkey breast with the pork fat or bacon, tie with kitchen twine, and season with salt and pepper. Generously brush a roasting pan with oil, put the turkey in it, and roast in the oven for 1½ hours, basting occasionally.

Remove the pork fat or bacon, return the turkey to the oven, and roast for another 30 minutes, or until browned, cooked through, and tender. Remove the turkey from the roasting pan and let rest for 10 minutes, then place in a warm serving dish and serve.

Rotolo di tacchino al passito con carote

Turkey Roulade in Passito Wine with Carrots

Serves 4
Preparation: 20 minutes, plus
    cooling time
Cooking: 1 hour, plus
    5 minutes resting

3 tablespoons butter
1 leek, trimmed and cut into rings
3½ oz/100 g sausage, casing
    removed and meat crumbled
5 sage leaves, cut into strips
¾ cup (1½ oz/40 g) fresh
    bread crumbs
1 egg
1¾ lb/800 g turkey breast,
    butterflied
½ cup (4 fl oz/120 ml) Passito wine
1 lb 2 oz/500 g carrots, cut
    into sticks
½ cup (4 fl oz/120 ml) hot
    vegetable broth (stock)
salt and pepper

Photograph opposite

Preheat the oven to 350°F/180°C/Gas Mark 4. Melt 2 teaspoons of the butter in a flameproof Dutch oven (casserole) over low heat. Add the leek and sausage and brown for 5 minutes. Add 2 sage leaves, then season with salt and pepper and let cool.

Add the bread crumbs and egg to the cooled leek mixture and mix together. Lay the butterflied turkey on a sheet of parchment paper, cover evenly with the mixture, roll it up, and tie the meat with kitchen twine.

Melt the remaining butter in a Dutch oven over high heat, add the turkey, and cook for about 10 minutes, or until browned all over. Pour in the wine and let it evaporate gently. Add the carrots, hot broth (stock), and remaining sage leaves. Season with salt and cook in the oven for 40 minutes.

Remove the meat from the oven, let rest for 5 minutes, then remove the kitchen twine. Carve the meat into slices and serve with the carrots and cooking juices.

Note: If the turkey breast is more than ½ inch/1 cm thick, lay the meat between 2 sheets of parchment paper and pound with a meat tenderizer until a thinner, even slice is achieved.

Cosce di tacchino con salsa al sedano
Turkey Thighs in Celery Sauce

Serves 4
Preparation: 20 minutes, plus
   10 minutes soaking
Cooking: 50 minutes

scant ¼ cup (1 oz/30 g) raisins
4 turkey thighs
2 tablespoons butter
2 shallots, sliced
½ cup (4 fl oz/120 ml) white wine
1 head celery, trimmed, outer
   stalks discarded, and thinly
   sliced, tender leaves, coarsely
   chopped and set aside
2 sprigs thyme, tied with
   kitchen twine
2 slices speck, diced
scant ½ cup (3½ fl oz/100 ml)
   vegetable broth (stock)
salt and pepper
Potato Rösti (page 284),
   to serve

Photograph opposite

Soak the raisins in a bowl of warm water for 10 minutes. Drain and dry. Preheat the oven to 350°F/180°C/Gas Mark 4.

Season the turkey thighs with salt. Melt the butter in a flameproof Dutch oven (casserole), add the turkey thighs, and sear, turning frequently, for about 5 minutes, or until browned on all sides. Add the shallots and white wine and simmer for about 5 minutes, or until it has slightly reduced. Add the celery, thyme, and diced speck. Pour in the broth (stock) and cook in the oven for 40 minutes.

Arrange the thighs in a warm serving dish. Remove the thyme from the cooking juices and discard. Blend the juices in a food processor or using a handheld blender until it is a smooth, creamy sauce. Add the raisins and a generous grind of pepper. Serve the turkey with the sauce, the reserved chopped celery leaves, and potato rösti.

Spezzatino alla senape
Turkey Stew with Mustard

Serves 4
Preparation: 2¼ hours
Cooking: 1 hour 5 minutes

2 tablespoons olive oil
2 tablespoons butter
1 onion, chopped
1 clove garlic, chopped
1 lb 5 oz/600 g skinless, boneless
   turkey breast, cut into cubes
¾ cup (6 fl oz/175 ml) dry
   white wine
1 cup (8 fl oz/250 ml) hot chicken
   broth (stock)
2 tablespoons Dijon mustard
1 sprig flat-leaf parsley, chopped
salt and pepper

Heat the oil and butter in a large skillet (frying pan), add the onion and garlic, and cook over low heat for 5 minutes, stirring occasionally. Increase the heat to medium, add the turkey, and cook, stirring frequently, for 10 minutes, or until golden brown. Season with salt and pepper, pour in the wine, and cook until it has evaporated. Pour in ¾ cup (6 fl oz/175 ml) of the hot broth (stock), cover, and simmer for 30 minutes.

Combine the remaining broth and the mustard in a bowl and stir into the skillet. Sprinkle the stew with the parsley and simmer for another 15 minutes. Serve.

Sides

Although meat is almost always the main event in Italian cooking, vegetables play a vital supporting role. *Soffrito*—finely chopped onion, celery, garlic, and carrot softened in olive oil or butter—is the basis of myriad dishes. Herbs are equally important, adding depth of flavor, aroma, and color, from the ubiquitous basil and flat-leaf parsley to woodier Mediterranean stalwarts, such as thyme, rosemary, and sage.

Perhaps the most important vegetable in Italian cooking is not a vegetable at all but a fruit—the tomato. Ripened in the Italian sun, these luscious fruits bear little resemblance to the rock hard, watery versions found in US grocery stores and UK supermarkets and they are the basis of many Italian dishes. Sliced, seasoned, and drizzled with good olive oil, or partnered with a creamy buffalo mozzarella, it's a dish in itself. And when puréed—*passata di pomodoro*—tomatoes really enhance the richness and flavor of silky stewed or braised meat dishes.

The aromatic anise-flavored fennel bulb adds both texture and flavor to any number of salads or baked dishes and works well with pork. It can be braised, fried (see page 258), roasted, or simply finely chopped into a salad with artichokes and capers (see page 257) or with fresh herbs, blood orange, and the wonderfully bitter radicchio.

Radicchio is the Italian name for several varieties of red chicory, some with pointed red leaves and broad, white ribs and others more variegated and cabbage shape. Their spectacular appearance, slightly bitter flavor, and crisp texture make them a welcome addition to winter salads. Radicchio is often cooked in Italy and may be baked, broiled, or coated with batter and deep-fried. When tossed in olive oil and sautéed (see page 254) or broiled (grilled) for 10 minutes, it makes an ideal accompaniment to any broiled or roasted meat. It can even be cooked with the meat, as shown in Beef Tenderloin with Radicchio (see page 62).

Puntarelle, a variety of chicory with serrated leaves, is picked when it is young and tender and may be enjoyed either raw or cooked. Its slightly bitter flavor—softened when sautéed in butter—pairs well with rich and hearty meat dishes.

Vibrant peas are a great accompaniment to meats, such as duck or chicken, and are often added directly to stews or cooked with pancetta for added flavor (see page 262). They work well with any meat, game, and poultry dishes.

White or green beans can be served with pesto, stirred into cream and Parmesan, or sautéed in butter, garlic, and chile (chilli), see page 260. Broccoli works equally well with these flavor combinations, particularly broccolini (purple sprouting broccoli) and is an excellent and nutritious accompaniment to meat dishes.

Bell peppers are popular and versatile, their sweetness provides a lovely counterpoint when stuffed with lamb or pork, and they can be sautéed, roasted, fried, or baked. Southern Italy's *peperonata* (see page 270) is a classic and peppers are its star ingredient. Slowly cooked with tomatoes, onions, and garlic into an intensely silky stew, it works equally well accompanying roasted meat or poultry, such as Roasted Goose with Sweet-and-Sour Bell Peppers (see page 224). It also tastes great stirred through pasta or generously spooned onto a thick slice of bread.

Brussels sprouts may not be traditional in the Italian kitchen, but they are starting to become more popular. They are often simply blanched and then sautéed with pancetta, but they also work well when puréed (see page 276). Brussels sprouts pair well with sweet nuts, such as chestnuts and almonds, and warm spices, such as nutmeg. They are a delicious accompaniment to pork, game, and poultry, and taste wonderful when braised in the cooking juices of roasted meat.

Insalatina mista alle erbe aromatiche

Mixed Salad with Aromatic Herbs

Serves 4
Preparation: 5 minutes

5 oz/150 g mixed salad greens
   (leaves), such as mint, wild
   fennel, parsley, and basil
1 tablespoon balsamic vinegar
4 tablespoons olive oil
salt

Arrange the mixed salad greens (leaves) in a salad bowl. Mix the vinegar, olive oil, and a pinch of salt together in a small bowl, then drizzle over the salad. Serve.

Radicchio tardivo in padella

Sautéed Radicchio

Serves 4
Preparation: 5 minutes
Cooking: 10 minutes

1½ tablespoons butter
3 heads radicchio tardivo,
   outer leaves removed and
   cut into pieces
1 shallot, chopped
grated zest of 1 orange
1 tablespoon apple cider vinegar
salt

Photograph opposite

Heat the butter in a skillet (frying pan), add the radicchio, chopped shallot, grated orange zest, and the vinegar, and season with a pinch of salt. Sauté for 10 minutes or until tender. Remove the skillet from the heat, transfer the radicchio to a warm serving dish, and serve.

Catalogna al burro e parmigiano

Puntarelle with Parmesan and Butter

Serves 4
Preparation: 5 minutes
Cooking: 10 minutes

2 heads puntarelle, trimmed and
    cut into small pieces
3 tablespoons butter
1 clove garlic, chopped
generous ⅓ cup (1 oz/30 g) freshly
    grated Parmesan cheese
salt

Bring a pan of salted water to a boil, add the puntarelle, and boil for 5–6 minutes, then drain. Melt the butter in a skillet (frying pan), add the puntarelle, garlic, and Parmesan, and sauté for about 5 minutes, or until the puntarelle is cooked. Remove the skillet from the heat, transfer the puntarelle to a warm serving dish, and serve.

Catalogna ripassata in padella

Sautéed Puntarelle

Serves 4
Preparation: 5 minutes
Cooking: 10 minutes

11 oz/300 g puntarelle, trimmed
    and cut into small pieces
4 tablespoons olive oil
1 clove garlic, chopped
salt and pepper

Photograph page 93

Bring a pan of salted water to a boil, add the puntarelle, and boil for 5–6 minutes, then drain. Heat the oil in a skillet (frying pan), add the puntarelle and garlic, and season with a grind of pepper. Sauté for about 5 minutes, or until the puntarelle is cooked. Remove the skillet from the heat, transfer the puntarelle to a warm serving dish, and serve.

Insalata riccia saltata in padella

Sautéed Escarole

Serves 4
Preparation: 10 minutes
Cooking: 5 minutes

4 tablespoons olive oil
1 clove garlic
1 escarole, outer leaves removed
    and finely chopped
salt

Heat the oil in a skillet (frying pan) over medium heat, add the escarole, garlic clove, and a pinch of salt and sauté for 4–5 minutes, or until the escarole is cooked and all the water has evaporated. Remove the skillet from the heat, transfer the escarole to a warm serving dish, and serve.

Insalata di finocchi e carciofi

Fennel and Artichoke Salad

Serves 4
Preparation: 30 minutes

½ cup (4 fl oz/120 ml) olive oil
juice of 1 orange, strained
3 fennel bulbs
juice of 1 lemon, strained
2 globe artichokes
1 tablespoon small capers,
    drained and rinsed
salt and pepper

Whisk together the oil and orange juice in a small bowl and season with salt and pepper. Set aside.

Remove the tough outer layers of the fennel and cut out the cores, then slice very thinly, preferably using a mandoline.

Fill a bowl halfway with water and stir in the lemon juice. Trim the artichoke stems, remove any coarse leaves and the chokes, and cut the artichokes into small pieces, then add the pieces immediately to the acidulated water to prevent discoloration.

Drain the artichokes thoroughly and put into a salad bowl. Add the fennel and sprinkle with the capers. Finally, drizzle the oil and orange dressing over the salad and serve.

Finocchi fritti

Fried Fennel

Serves 4
Preparation: 15 minutes
Cooking: 20 minutes

juice of 1 lemon
4 bulbs fennel
2 sprigs marjoram, leaves chopped
2 sprigs thyme, leaves chopped
1 tablespoon grated Parmesan
    or pecorino cheese
olive oil, for drizzling and
    deep-frying
all-purpose (plain) flour, to roll
2 eggs, beaten
bread crumbs, to roll
vegetable oil, for frying
salt and pepper
fennel fronds, to garnish (optional)
lemon wedges, to garnish
    (optional)

Photograph opposite

Fill a bowl halfway with water and stir in the lemon juice. Remove the tough outer layers of the fennel bulbs and cut each one into 8 wedges. Drop the wedges immediately into the acidulated water.

Bring a pan of lightly salted water to a boil and blanch the fennel for 7–8 minutes. Drain and pat dry with paper towels. Arrange the fennel wedges in a large dish and season with salt and pepper. Sprinkle over the chopped marjoram and thyme together with the grated cheese, then drizzle with oil.

Spread the flour out on a plate, put the beaten eggs into a shallow bowl, and spread the bread crumbs out on another plate. Roll the fennel wedges first in the flour, then in the beaten eggs, and finally in the bread crumbs.

Heat enough oil for deep-frying in a deep fryer or deep skillet (frying pan) to 350°F/180°C, or until a cube of bread browns in 30 seconds. Deep-fry the wedges of fennel until golden brown. Remove with a slotted spoon and drain on paper towels. Transfer to a warm serving dish, garnish with fennel fronds and some lemon wedges, if using, and serve.

Note: This side dish works particularly well with roasted pork.

Fagiolini olio e aglio

Green Beans with Oil and Garlic

Serves 4
Preparation: 10 minutes
Cooking: 5–6 minutes

4 tablespoons olive oil
11 oz/300 g green (French) beans,
  cut into thin slices diagonally
1 clove garlic, crushed
1 hot chile (chilli), diced

Photograph opposite

Heat the oil in a skillet (frying pan) over medium heat, add the green (French) beans, 2 tablespoons water, the garlic, and chile (chilli), and sauté for 5–6 minutes, or until cooked. Remove the skillet from the heat, transfer the green beans to a warm serving dish, and serve.

Purè di piselli alla noce moscata

Pea Purée with Nutmeg

Serves 4
Preparation: 5 minutes
Cooking: 5–10 minutes

3½ cups (1 lb 2 oz/500 g) peas
3 tablespoons butter
pinch of grated nutmeg
salt and pepper

Bring a pan of salted water to a boil, add the peas, and boil over high heat for 5–10 minutes, or until tender. Drain and blend with the butter, a pinch of salt, a grind of pepper, and the nutmeg in a food processor or using a handheld blender until smooth. Transfer to a warm serving dish and serve.

Purè di piselli al profumo di menta

Pea Purée with Mint

Serves 4
Preparation: 10 minutes
Cooking: 5–10 minutes

3¾ cups (1 lb 2oz/500 g) frozen
  peas
3 tablespoons butter
pinch of grated nutmeg
2–3 mint leaves
salt

Bring a pan of salted water to a boil, add the peas, and boil over high heat for 5–10 minutes, or until tender. Drain and blend with the butter, a pinch of salt, the nutmeg, and mint leaves in a food processor or using a handheld blender until smooth. Transfer to a warm serving dish, and serve.

Piselli alla pancetta

Peas with Pancetta

Serves 4
Preparation: 50 minutes
Cooking: 15–20 minutes

2¼ lb/1 kg fresh peas, shelled
  (about 2¼ cups shelled)
3 tablespoons butter
3½ oz/100 g smoked pancetta,
  cut into strips
salt

Bring a pan of salted water to a boil, add the peas, and boil over high heat for 5–10 minutes, or until tender, then drain well and set aside.

Melt the butter in a pan over low heat, add the pancetta, and cook until golden brown and tender. Add the peas and cook, stirring occasionally, for 5 minutes. Remove the pan from the heat, transfer the peas and pancetta to a warm serving dish, and serve.

Topinambur in padella

Sautéed Jerusalem Artichokes

Serves 4
Preparation: 15 minutes
Cooking: 15 minutes

1 lb 2 oz/500 g Jerusalem
    artichokes
2 tablespoons butter
salt and pepper

Photograph page 151

Peel the Jerusalem artichokes and cut into ¼-inch/5-mm thick slices. Bring a pan of water to a boil, add the artichokes, and blanch for 10 minutes, then drain.

Melt the butter in a skillet (frying pan), add the artichokes, a pinch of salt, and a grind of pepper, and sauté until golden brown. Remove the skillet from the heat, transfer the artichokes to a warm serving dish, and serve.

Asparagi alla senape dolce

Asparagus with Sweet Mustard

Serves 4
Preparation: 10 minutes
Cooking: 10–12 minutes

2 bunches of asparagus, trimmed
    and cleaned
4 tablespoons olive oil

For the dressing:
4 tablespoons olive oil
sweet mustard, to taste
salt

Bring a pan of water to a boil, add the asparagus, and blanch for 5 minutes, then drain. Preheat a ridged grill pan (griddle). Coat the asparagus with the oil and cook on the hot grill pan for 5–6 minutes, or until tender. Remove the asparagus from the grill pan, cut into small pieces, and place in a warm serving dish.

Make the dressing by whisking the sweet mustard, oil, and a pinch of salt together in a small bowl. Pour the dressing over the asparagus and serve.

Purè di cavolfiore

Cauliflower Purée

Serves 4
Preparation: 20 minutes
Cooking: 30 minutes

1 lb 8½ oz/700 g cauliflower
(1 medium head), cut into
small florets
7 oz/200 g potatoes, cut into
medium wedges
2¼ cups (17 fl oz/500 ml) milk
pinch of grated nutmeg
salt and pepper

Cut the cauliflower florets in half and put into a Dutch oven (casserole) with the potato wedges. Add 2¼ cups (17 fl oz/500 ml) water and a pinch of salt, and bring to a boil. Cover, reduce the heat, and simmer for 20 minutes. Remove from the heat and blend all the ingredients in a food processor. Add the milk and blend again until it is a creamy consistency.

Transfer to the Dutch oven and heat over medium heat, making sure the purée doesn't boil. After 5–10 minutes, remove from the heat and season with salt and pepper and a pinch of nutmeg. Transfer to a warm serving dish and serve.

Note: This purée works well as a side dish to roasted meat.

Purè di sedano rapa

Mashed Celery Root

Serves 4
Preparation: 30 minutes
Cooking: 25 minutes

14 oz/400 g celery root (celeriac),
peeled and diced
scant ½ cup (3½ fl oz/100 ml)
sour cream
salt

Photograph page 163

Bring a pan of salted water to a boil, add the celery root (celeriac), and boil for 5–6 minutes, or until tender. Drain and return to the pan. Add the sour cream, a pinch of salt, and a grind of pepper, and blend with a handheld blender until smooth. Transfer to a warm serving dish and serve.

Note: This mash is a great accompaniment to rabbit.

Melanzane violette ala griglia

Grilled Violet Eggplants

Serves 4
Preparation 10 minutes
Cooking: 4–6 minutes

3 violet eggplants (aubergines),
   stems removed and flesh cut
   into ¼-inch/½-cm slices
4–5 tablespoons olive oil
few basil leaves, chopped
salt

Preheat a ridged grill pan (griddle). Put the eggplant (aubergine) slices onto the hot grill pan and grill for 2–3 minutes on each side. Transfer to a warm serving dish and sprinkle with a pinch of salt. Drizzle with the oil, garnish with chopped basil leaves, and serve.

Nastri di zucchine al pepe rosa

Zucchini Ribbons with Pink Peppercorns

Serves 4
Preparation: 10 minutes
Cooking: 5 minutes

1 lb 2 oz/500 g zucchini
   (courgettes), sliced into ribbons
olive oil, to drizzle
pink peppercorns, crushed,
   to taste
salt

Photograph opposite

Bring a pan of salted water to a boil, add the zucchini (courgette) ribbons, and blanch for a few seconds, then drain well. Place in a warm serving dish and drizzle with oil. Sprinkle with crushed pink peppercorns, season with salt, and serve.

Zucchine, patate e pomodori al forno

Roasted Zucchini, Potatoes, and Tomatoes

Serves 4
Preparation: 20 minutes
Cooking: 1 hour

1 lb/450 g potatoes, cut into
   chunks
1 onion, chopped
1 clove garlic
olive oil, for drizzling
1 sprig rosemary, chopped
1 lb 7 oz/650 g zucchini
   (courgettes), diced
11 oz/300 g tomatoes, coarsely
   chopped (about 1¾ cups)
salt and pepper

Photograph opposite

Preheat the oven to 375°F/190°C/Gas Mark 5. Put the potatoes into an ovenproof dish, add the chopped onion and the garlic clove, and season with salt and pepper. Drizzle with the olive oil and sprinkle with the rosemary. Roast for 40 minutes, then remove from the oven but do not turn off the oven.

Remove and discard the garlic. Add the diced zucchini (courgettes) and chopped tomatoes to the dish, lightly season with salt, and stir. Return the dish to the oven and roast for another 20 minutes, or until the vegetables are tender. Serve.

Insalata, mais e peperone rosso

Corn and Red Bell Pepper Salad

Serves 4
Preparation: 10 minutes

1 head curly leafed lettuce
1 cup (6 oz/175 g) canned corn
   kernels, drained
1 red bell pepper, cored, seeded,
   and cut into strips
salt and pepper

Arrange the lettuce in a salad bowl, sprinkle with the corn kernels, and add the red bell pepper strips. Season to taste with salt and pepper. Serve.

Peperonata delicata

Delicate Peperonata

Serves 4
Preparation: 15 minutes
Cooking: 1½ hours, plus
    cooling time

4 mixed bell peppers
4 tablespoons olive oil
1 clove garlic
1 onion, sliced
4 tomatoes, peeled, seeded,
    and chopped
salt

Photograph opposite

Preheat the oven to 350°F/180°C/Gas Mark 4. Line a roasting pan with kitchen foil. Prick the bell peppers with a fork, put into the pan, and roast in the oven for 1 hour. Remove from the oven, cover with kitchen foil, and let cool.

Halve the bell peppers, remove the seeds and membranes, and cut the bell peppers into large strips. Heat the oil in a pan with the garlic clove. Add the bell pepper strips and sliced onion and cook over low heat, stirring occasionally, for 10 minutes. Add the tomatoes, season with salt, and cook for 20 minutes, or until thickened.

Remove and discard the garlic before transferring to a warm serving dish. Serve.

Peperoni abbrustoliti al rosmarino

Roasted Peppers with Rosemary

Serves 4
Preparation: 10 minutes
Cooking: 25–30 minutes

4 red bell peppers, halved,
    cored, and seeded
2 tablespoons olive oil
1 tablespoon balsamic vinegar
1 sprig rosemary, leaves
    finely chopped
salt

Preheat the oven to 400°F/200°C/Gas Mark 6. Put the bell pepper halves, cut side up, onto a baking sheet and roast in the oven for 25–30 minutes, or until tender.

Remove the bell peppers from the oven and let cool. Once cool enough to handle, cut them into thin strips. Place the bell pepper strips in a warm serving dish and dress with the oil and vinegar. Sprinkle with a pinch of salt and the chopped rosemary and serve.

Broccoletti al peperoncino

Broccolini with Chile

Serves 4
Preparation: 10 minutes
Cooking: 10 minutes

1 lb 2 oz/500 g broccolini
  (tenderstem broccoli), outer
  leaves discarded and cut
  into florets
2–3 tablespoons olive oil
½ fresh red chile (chilli), seeded
  and finely sliced
salt

Photograph opposite

Bring a pan of salted water to a boil, add the broccolini (tenderstem broccoli), and blanch for 5 minutes, then drain. Heat some oil in a skillet (frying pan), add the broccolini and sliced red chile (chilli), season with salt, and sauté until tender. Remove the skillet from the heat, transfer the broccolini to a warm serving dish, and serve.

Carote glassate

Glazed Carrots

Serves 4
Preparation: 15 minutes
Cooking time: 20 minutes

1¾ lb/800 g new season carrots,
  cut into circles
1 heaping tablespoon superfine
  (caster) sugar
4½ tablespoons butter
2 sprigs mint, chopped
salt

Put the carrots into a Dutch oven (casserole), add the sugar, salt, and butter and cover everything with plenty of cold water. Place over medium heat and cook for 20 minutes, shaking the Dutch oven now and then so that the carrots do not stick to the bottom of the pan. When the cooking time is up, the liquid will have evaporated, leaving a delicious, sugary glaze. Sprinkle with the chopped mint and serve.

Note: Glazed carrots are a very special side dish. Pleasantly sweet, they are the ideal accompaniment to roasted chicken, broiled (grilled) sausages, or roasted beef.

Carote al miele d'acacia

Carrots with Acacia Honey

Serves 4
Preparation: 15 minutes
Cooking: 25 minutes

7 tablespoons butter
1¾ lb/800 g carrots, thickly sliced
1 tablespoon acacia honey
scant ½ cup (3½ fl oz/100 ml)
    brandy
2 tablespoons chopped parsley
salt

Photograph opposite

Melt the butter in a lidded skillet (frying pan). Add the carrots and cook over medium heat, stirring occasionally, for a few minutes. Season with salt and stir again, then stir in the honey. Cover and cook, stirring occasionally, for about 20 minutes, or until tender. If the pan starts to dry out, add a little hot water.

Toward the end of the cooking time, sprinkle the brandy over the carrots and cook until the alcohol has evaporated. Remove the skillet from the heat and transfer the carrots to a warm serving dish. Sprinkle with the chopped parsley and serve.

Note: This is an ideal accompaniment to roasted veal, poultry, or rabbit.

Carote al profumo di coriandolo

Carrots with Cilantro

Serves 4
Preparation: 10 minutes
Cooking: 5–10 minutes

4 tablespoons olive oil
14 oz/400 g carrots, cut
    into matchsticks
1 clove garlic, crushed
cilantro (coriander) leaves,
    chopped
salt

Heat the oil in a skillet (frying pan) over medium heat, add the carrot sticks, the crushed garlic, and a pinch of salt. Cook for 5–10 minutes, or until tender. Remove the skillet from the heat and transfer the carrots to a warm serving dish. Serve the carrots sprinkled with chopped cilantro (coriander) leaves.

Purè di cavolini di bruxelles

Puréed Brussels Sprouts

Serves 6
Preparation: 15 minutes
Cooking: 25–30 minutes

2¼ lb/1 kg Brussels sprouts
2 tablespoons butter
4 tablespoons heavy (double)
   cream
pinch of grated nutmeg
salt and white pepper
Parmesan shavings, to sprinkle
   (optional)
extra virgin olive oil, to drizzle
   (optional)

Photograph opposite

Bring a pan of water to a boil, add the Brussels sprouts, and boil for 10–15 minutes, or until just tender. Drain, transfer to a food processor, and blend until it is a smooth, fluffy kind of cream. Put the mixture into a clean saucepan, add the butter and cream, and cook over medium heat for 15 minutes, or until it thickens.

Remove the pan from the heat and transfer the purée to a warm serving dish. Season with salt, white pepper, and a pinch of nutmeg. Sprinkle with some Parmesan shavings and drizzle with oil, if using, and serve.

Note: Serve as a side dish with roasted meat or pan-fried sausages.

Cavolini di bruxelles alla pancetta

Brussels Sprouts with Pancetta

Serves 4
Preparation: 5 minutes
Cooking: 15 minutes

14 oz/400 g Brussels sprouts
3 tablespoons olive oil
1½ oz/40 g smoked pancetta,
   sliced

Bring a pan of water to a boil, add the Brussels sprouts, boil for 10 minutes, then drain. Heat the oil in a skillet (frying pan), add the Brussels sprouts and pancetta, and fry for about 5 minutes, or until the pancetta is crispy. Remove the pan from the heat, transfer the sprouts and pancetta to a warm serving dish, and serve.

Cavolini di bruxelles alla parmigiana

Parmesan Brussels Sprouts

Serves 4
Preparation time: 15 minutes
Cooking time: 20 minutes

1¾ lb/800 g Brussels sprouts,
    trimmed
2 tablespoons butter
pinch of freshly grated nutmeg
2½ oz/65 g Parmesan cheese,
    grated (about ¾ cup)
salt and pepper

Bring a pan of water to a boil, add the Brussels sprouts, cook for 10 minutes, then drain. Melt the butter in a skillet (frying pan) over low heat until golden brown. Add the Brussels sprouts and cook for a few minutes. Season with salt and pepper to taste and add a pinch of nutmeg. Transfer to a warm serving dish, sprinkle with the Parmesan, and serve.

Cavolo rosso caramellato

Caramelized Red Cabbage

Serves 8
Preparation: 15 minutes
Cooking: 1 hour 10 minutes

2¼ lb/1 kg red cabbage, cut
    into thin slices
scant ¼ cup (1¾ fl oz/50 ml)
    white wine vinegar
2 tablespoons superfine (caster)
    sugar
salt and pepper

Put the cabbage into a Dutch oven (casserole), pour in scant ½ cup (3½ fl oz/100 ml) water with the vinegar and sugar, then season with salt and pepper. Bring to a boil, reduce the heat, cover with the lid, and cook for 1 hour, stirring frequently during the last 30 minutes. At this stage, the liquid should have evaporated and the cabbage should be lightly caramelized.

Remove the Dutch oven from the heat, transfer the cabbage to a warm serving dish, and serve.

Note: Serve hot or cold with roasted pork dishes.

Cavolo rosso stufato al cumino

Stewed Red Cabbage with Cumin

Serves 4
Preparation: 10 minutes
Cooking: 35 minutes

1 red cabbage
2 tablespoons butter
pinch of ground cumin
1 onion, finely chopped
1 cup (8 fl oz/250 ml) vegetable
  broth (stock)
salt

Remove and discard the outer leaves from the cabbage and cut into very fine strips. Melt the butter in a deep skillet (frying pan), add the cabbage, cumin, chopped onion, vegetable broth (stock), and a pinch of salt, and cook for about 35 minutes, or until the cabbage is tender. Remove the skillet from the heat, transfer the cabbage to a warm serving dish, and serve.

Purè di patate e cavolo

Mashed Potatoes and Cabbage

Serves 4
Preparation: 15 minutes
Cooking: 30 minutes

1 lb 2 oz/500 g potatoes, unpeeled
2 tablespoons butter
½ green or white cabbage, cut
  into thin strips
salt

Bring a large saucepan of water to a boil, add the unpeeled potatoes, and boil for about 30 minutes, or until tender and cooked through. Once cooked, drain, remove the skin, return the potatoes to the pan, and mash with a potato masher.

Meanwhile, melt the butter in another pan, add the cabbage, a pinch of salt, and ⅔ cup (5 fl oz/150 ml) water, and cook for 20 minutes. Blend the cabbage in a food processor, then mix with the mashed potatoes. Transfer the mash to a warm serving dish and serve.

Purè di patate cremoso

Creamy Mashed Potatoes

Serves 4
Preparation: 25 minutes
Cooking: 25–30 minutes

6 potatoes
4 tablespoons butter, softened
scant ½ cup (3½ fl oz/100 ml) milk
scant ½ cup (3½ oz/100 g)
  mascarpone cheese
½ cup (4 fl oz/120 ml) light (single)
  cream
6 chives, chopped
salt and pepper

Photograph opposite

Steam the potatoes for about 20 minutes, then pass through a potato ricer into a bowl. Gently stir in the butter.

In a small saucepan, heat the milk to just below simmering point, then remove from the heat. Beat together the mascarpone and cream until smooth in another bowl, then stir in the hot milk and pour the mixture over the potatoes. Mix well, season with salt and pepper to taste, and press the mixture through a strainer (sieve) into a warm serving dish. Sprinkle with the chives and serve.

Note: This mashed potato is quite loose. If you prefer a firmer consistency, leave out the cream. This will also make it less rich.

Purè di patate alla noce moscata

Mashed Potatoes with Nutmeg

Serves 4
Preparation: 20 minutes
Cooking: 25–35 minutes

1¾ lb/800 g potatoes, unpeeled
pat (knob) of butter
scant ½ cup (3½ fl oz/100 ml)
  milk, warmed
pinch of grated nutmeg
salt

Bring a large saucepan of water to a boil, add the unpeeled potatoes, and cook for 20–30 minutes, or until tender and cooked through. Drain and peel them while they are still hot. Return to the pan and mash with a potato masher. Add the butter and warm milk and put over low heat for 3–4 minutes.

Remove the pan from the heat and transfer the mashed potatoes to a warm serving dish. Season with a pinch each of salt and nutmeg and serve.

Purè di patate al lime

Mashed Potatoes with Lime

Serves 4
Preparation 15 minutes
Cooking 20–30 minutes

1¾ lb/800 g potatoes, unpeeled
3½ tablespoons olive oil
zest and juice of 1 unwaxed lime
salt

Bring a large saucepan of water to a boil, add the unpeeled potatoes, and cook for 20–30 minutes, or until tender and cooked through. Once cooked, drain, remove the skin, return to the pan, and mash with a potato masher. Mix in the olive oil, the lime juice and zest, and a pinch of salt. Transfer the mashed potatoes to a warm serving dish and serve.

Patate arrosto croccanti

Crunchy Roasted Potatoes

Serves 4
Preparation: 10 minutes
Cooking: 40 minutes

1½ lb/675 g potatoes, unpeeled
2 tablespoons butter
3 tablespoons olive oil
salt

Bring a large saucepan of water to a boil, add the unpeeled potatoes, and boil for 20–30 minutes, or until tender. Drain and set aside to cool. Peel the cooled potatoes, cut into wedges, and roast in a skillet (frying pan) with the butter and oil until golden brown. Remove the skillet from the heat, transfer the potatoes to a warm serving dish, and serve.

Patatine novelle al rosmarino

New Potatoes With Rosemary

Serves 4
Preparation: 10 minutes
Cooking: 30–35 minutes

2 tablespoons butter
scant ½ cup (3½ fl oz/100 ml) olive oil
1 sprig rosemary
1 clove garlic
1½ lb/675 g new potatoes
salt

Photograph opposite

Heat the butter and oil in a large pan, add the rosemary, garlic, and new potatoes, stir, and cover. Cook over low heat for 30–35 minutes, or until golden brown. Remove the pan from the heat and transfer the potatoes to a warm serving dish. Remove and discard the garlic, sprinkle the potatoes with salt, and serve.

Patate alla griglia

Grilled Potatoes

Serves 4
Preparation: 10 minutes
Cooking: 10–12 minutes

4–5 potatoes, peeled and cut
    into slices ¼ inch/5 mm thick
3 tablespoons olive oil
salt

Preheat a ridged grill pan (griddle). Bring a pan of salted water to a boil and blanch the sliced potatoes for 5 minutes, then drain. Add the oil and a pinch of salt. Put the potatoes onto the grill pan and grill for 2–3 minutes on each side, turning once only. Transfer to a warm serving dish and serve.

Tortino di rösti di patate

Potato Rösti

Serves 4
Preparation: 10 minutes, plus
    20 minutes cooling
Cooking: 30 minutes

1 lb 2 oz/500 g potatoes, unpeeled
3 tablespoons butter
salt

Bring a pan of salted water to a boil, add the whole potatoes, and boil for 10 minutes, then drain and let cool. Once the potatoes are cool, peel and coarsely grate them with a grater. Season with salt.

Melt 1½ tablespoons of the butter in a nonstick skillet (frying pan). Add the grated potatoes to the pan and gently push down with a spatula (fish slice) to make a compact cake. Cook over low heat until golden brown and crispy. Remove the rösti from the pan with the help of the lid.

Melt the remaining butter in the pan and return the rösti to the pan the other way up. Cook for another 10 minutes. Remove the skillet from the heat and transfer the rösti to a warm serving dish. Cut into slices and serve.

Polenta

Polenta

Serves 6
Cooking: 45–60 minutes

3⅔ cups (1 lb 2 oz/500 g) polenta
   or cornmeal
7½ cups (60 fl oz/1.7 liters) water

Bring a large saucepan of salted water to a boil and keep another pot of water boiling in case it is needed. Sprinkle the polenta into the pan while stirring continuously and reduce the heat to the low. Continue to stir and as soon as the polenta thickens, soften it with a drop of the reserved hot water. This is the secret to cooking polenta successfully, because polenta thickens with the application of heat and softens with the addition of water.

The cooking time ranges from 45 minutes to 1 hour; the longer the cooking time the more easily the polenta is digested.

Note: Polenta must be kept dry, otherwise it turns moldy. Cooked polenta should be stored wrapped in a clean dish towel in the bottom of the refrigerator. Soft polenta works well when served with stews and braised meat.

Purè di lenticchie alla salvia

Puréed Lentils with Sage

Serves 4
Preparation: 5 minutes
Cooking: 30 minutes

2½ cups (1 lb 2 oz/500 g) lentils
2 tablespoons butter
4 sage leaves
salt and pepper

Follow the package directions to cook the lentils in a pan of boiling water until tender. Drain and while they are still hot, blend them in a food processor or with a handheld blender with the butter, a pinch of salt, a grind of pepper, and the sage leaves until puréed. Transfer to a warm serving dish and serve.

Note: Lentils work really well when paired with wild boar.

Glossary
and Index

Glossary

Acacia honey

A monofloral honey made from nectar collected from the delicate blossoms of the black locust or false acacia tree (*Robinia pseudoacacia*). Light in color, it has a mild, sweet, and floral flavor.

Agrodolce

This sweet-and-sour dressing made with herbs, wine vinegar, sugar, onion, and garlic is served with fish, game, and vegetables, particularly onions and eggplant (aubergine).

Anurka apple

A very old variety of apple that is native to Campania in Southern Italy. With red, rusty colored skin, it is firm, crisp, and sweet. It is fragrant and pleasantly acidulous. Also called "Annurca."

To bake in a package

To wrap food in kitchen foil, parchment paper, or wax paper and bake in the oven. This method requires very little oil or fat and is excellent for meat, fish, and vegetables, because it retains the cooking juices and aroma.

To baste

To spoon over fat or liquid during roasting or cooking in order to help browning and keep the basted food moist.

To blanch

To part cook fruit or vegetables briefly in boiling water to make them softer or easier to peel or to whiten by soaking in milk or water.

To blend

To combine ingredients, by hand or with an electric mixer, food processor, or blender, until creamy and evenly mixed.

To bone

To remove the bones from meat, poultry, or fish.

To braise

To cook slowly in a covered pan or Dutch oven (casserole) on low heat with a small quantity of liquid, usually specified in the recipe. Braising is mainly used for red meats, poultry, and game.

Broth

A flavored cooking liquid obtained by simmering beef, veal, or poultry bones with vegetables and herbs for 2–3 hours. Skim off the fat before use. For speed, a bouillon (stock) cube can be dissolved in hot water, and good liquid broth is also available in stores. Also known as stock.

To brown

A process also known as caramelization, browning involves cooking food over a high heat, usually by sautéing, roasting, grilling, or frying. The effect of searing enhances flavor and texture, particularly with meats, casseroles, or any dish that melts or crisps on top.

Cacciatore

Meaning "in the style of a hunter," this is a method of cooking chicken and/or rabbit with mushrooms, onions, white wine, herbs, and spices. There are many regional variations.

Cailletier olives

Known as "*olive Taggiasche*" in Italy, these olives are largely grown in Southern France and the Italian region of Liguria. Their color can range from a greenish purple hue to a brown black, and they have a sweet, fruity, and mild flavor. They can be eaten whole, ground into a spread, topped on meat, or pressed into oil.

Capon

A castrated, fattened rooster—where a large chicken will weigh 3–4 lb (1.4–1.8 kg), a capon can weigh 8–10 lb (3.6–4.5 kg) and is full of flavor. Capon carcasses are particularly good for broth (stock).

To chine

To cut meat across or along the backbone.

Cook over low heat

Dishes, such as stews, that require long cooking times to tenderize ingredients are cooked over low heat, that is, with the heat turned down to its lowest setting.

To cover

To seal a pan or dish with a lid or kitchen foil, either to shorten the cooking time or to slow down evaporation and prevent the ingredients from drying up.

To cut into portions

To cut poultry or game birds into serving pieces, using poultry shears or a very sharp knife.

To deglaze

To loosen carmelized sediment of food and dissolve the cooking juices produced in roasting pans and skillets with water, wine, or broth (stock) to make a gravy or sauce.

To dice

To cut vegetables, meat, or other ingredients into small, even cubes.

To draw

see To dress a bird

To dress a bird

Removing the feathers is a key stage in the process of preparing feathered game. The feathers are plucked from the tail upwards towards the head, and care is taken not to tear the skin. If the bird has been chilled in the refrigerator, plucking is the easiest option. Singeing removes the remaining down, leaving the residual "quills" that puncture beneath the skin's surface. These can be teased out with the help of a small knife.

To dust with flour

Meat, vegetables, and fish are often dusted—lightly coated—with flour before frying. Baking pans and counters are also dusted with flour to stop the dough from sticking.

To evaporate

To dry off an added liquid, such as broth (stock), wine, or liqueur, to give dishes extra flavor, usually by boiling.

Feathered game

Feathered game, a category including wild birds that are hunted and eaten, includes rock partridge, woodcock or snipe, grouse, pheasant, red grouse, and partridge. It also includes birds once caught in the wild that are now raised domestically, such as quail. The list of water birds includes wild duck, wild goose, mallard and teal, and wigeon.

Fricassée

A creamy sauce thickened with egg yolks and flavored with lemon poured onto veal, lamb, rabbit, or chicken. This dish must be removed from the heat as soon as it is ready, otherwise the sauce thickens excessively and may curdle.

Grappa

An alcoholic drink distilled from pomace—the grape skins, seeds, stalks, and pulp left over from the winemaking process. Traditionally enjoyed neat, after a meal, it can also be added to an after-dinner espresso for an extra kick. When used in meat and poultry dishes, such as Pork Loin with Apricot Sauce (see page 42), grappa can add a note of acidity to round out the flavors and cut the richness.

Grand Marnier

An orange-flavored liqueur produced in France and made from a blend of Cognac brandy, distilled essence of bitter orange, and sugar. It's made from a blend of Cognac, distilled essence of bitter orange and sugar. Often used in desserts, its orange flavor also combines well with chicken.

To hang

To store a whole animal or bird carcass for a length of time after butchering so that it becomes tender and succulent.

Juniper berry

A female seed cone produced by the various species of junipers. It is not a true berry but a cone with unusually fleshy and merged scales, which give it a berry-like appearance. It is spicy and aromatic, can be used fresh or dried.

To marinate

To place meat, game, or fish in an aromatic mixture, usually based on olive oil, lemon juice, vinegar, wine, spices, and herbs, in order to flavor and tenderize it.

Milanese

Meaning "from the city of Milan," this is a cooking method in which meat or vegetables are dipped in beaten egg and then coated with bread crumbs before sautéing. Milanese chops sautéed in butter are particularly famous.

Myrtle

A perennial shrub *Myrtus communis* has dark green leaves and purple-black colored berries. The leaves have a bitter taste and emit an aroma similar to that of juniper when crushed. As such they are used sparingly. Works well in meat dishes and can be used in place of bay leaves.

Myrtle liqueur

A traditional Sardinian liqueur made by infusing alcohol with myrtle berries. Known as *mirto* in Italian, it is reddish-brown in color and is sweet and fruity with herbal notes.

Pancetta

Cured pork taken from the belly of the pig, like lean bacon, but cured differently. It may be smoked or unsmoked, flat or rolled, and flavored with spices. It need to be cooked before being consumed. Thin slices can be wrapped around meat or poultry before cooking, while cubes can be added to a pan and sautéed with onions or garlic to add flavor. It is quite salty so it's best to taste before adding seasoning.

Partridge

The two most common types of partridge are the red-legged partridge and the grey. The rock partridge, which is highly prized gastronomically, is far more rare. Partridge meat is flavoursome and tender, and benefits from the bird having been hung for a few days to develop a gamey character.

Passate

Puréed canned tomatoes (passata), which are less concentrated than tomato paste (purée).

Passito wine

Italian sweet wine made from late-harvested grapes that have undergone a drying process. Typically served as a digestif, examples include vin santo and Passito di Pantelleria.

Pearl (baby) onions

Small onions—about 1 inch/2.5 cm in diameter—they come in red, white, or yellow. They have a mild, slightly sweet flavor. These onions can be difficult to peel, so it is best to put them in boiling water for 1-2 minutes, drain, and transfer to a bowl of cold water. Cut the root end and squeeze the onion out of its skin.

Pheasant

These birds are known for their lean, gamey meat. The cultivated variety, which are bred and released shortly before the hunting season, have less flavor than wild pheasant, and do not need to be hung. The meat pairs well with seasonal ingredients, including chestnuts, blueberries, squash, celery root (celeriac), cabbage, and mushrooms. Younger pheasants are ideal for roasting whole, whereas the older birds suit pies, casseroles, and stews. The sinewy legs tend to be tougher, so respond well to a slow braising process.

To pluck

see To dress a bird

Pork caul fat

A lacy, fatty membrane that encases the internal organs of animals such as cows, sheep, and pigs (the most common type of caul fat). Often used for wrapping patés or sausages, it comes in sheets and can be bought from most butchers.

Prosciutto

This is the Italian word for any kind of cured ham, including cooked ham. (*Prosciutto crudo* refers to raw, dry-cured ham, while *prosciutto cotto* refers to cooked ham.) However, in the United States, prosciutto is used to refer exclusively to raw, dry-cured ham, usually from Parma. Other fine versions of prosciutto are produced in Veneto and San Daniele.

Puntarelle

A type of Italian chicory, related to endive and radicchio. Long and spiky, its mild, bitter flavor is similar to arugula (rocket) but with the sweetness of fennel.

To purée

To reduce a solid or semi solid substance or mixture to a semiliquid or smooth cream, using a food processor or blender.

Quail

A small migratory bird, similar to a partridge, from the pheasant family. It is prized for its lean, delicately flavored meat. Preparation methods include marinating or wrapping the bird in pancetta to tenderize the meat preserve the moisture. Quails shot in the fall (autumn) months are round and plump and do not require hanging.

To reduce

To make a liquid, such as a broth (stock) or sauce, thicker and more concentrated by boiling it for longer.

To rest

To let meat sit out of the oven after roasting and before carving. As meat roasts, the muscle fibers contract, squeezing the juices towards the outer edges. During resting, the fibers relax, letting the juices redistribute within the meat, giving a more succulent result. Meat continues to cook during resting time, so always err on the side of caution with meat timings.

To roast

To cook meat, fish, or vegetables in the oven, on a spit, or in a pot (pot roast) after initially browning over high heat.

Rosata grapes

Grapes used for the Italian rosé wine known as *rosato*. There are four different Italian pink wines: Chiaretto, Ramato, Rosato, and Cerasuolo. Although Rosato is the general name for pink wines in Italy, it is also a category on its own.

Treviso raddichio

A mild variety of raddichio, Treviso is a vibrant lettuce also known as Italian red lettuce, or red chicory. It is distinguishable by its delicate crinkled leaves, deep magenta-purple color, and creamy white veins. It can be served fresh or cooked, its slightly bitter flavor mellowing after grilling, sautéing, or roasting, and it is packed with nutrients and antioxidants. Other types of chicory can be used as a substitute.

San Marzano tomatoes

A variety of Italian plum tomato originating from Naples. Thinner and more pointed than the Roma variety, the flesh of San Marzano tomatoes is much thicker and they have fewer seeds. They have a strong, sweet flavor with a delicate acidity that can balance out rich meats.

To sauté

To cook meat, fish, or vegetables in a skillet (frying pan) or sauté pan with oil or butter until browned and cooked through. Pasta and risotto may also be sautéed.

To simmer

To bring a liquid to just below boiling point or to turn down the heat under a liquid that has reached boiling point so that the surface of the liquid barely ripples.

Smoked lard

Lard, or *lardo* in Italian, is pork fat. Its subtle flavor and high smoking point make it good for roasting meat. The best quality lard is that made from fat found inside the loin and around the kidneys, known as flare or leaf fat. It is rendered then left to solidify into blocks of solid white fat. When smoked, it imparts a rich, smoky flavor.

Stewing chicken

Mature birds that are 15–16 months old. Their meat tends to be fairly tough and so requires prolonged cooking over low heat. Their rich flavor makes them perfect for soups and stews, as well as for making broth (stock). If making stock, it is best to remove the skin and underlying fat deposits before immersing the bird in lightly salted water. Cooking takes 1 hour or more, depending on the size of the bird. If the bird is old, it takes at least 2 hours. When the stock is ready, remove the fat by filtering it through a strainer lined with cheesecloth (muslin).

Strawberry tree honey

A honey made from nectar collected from the flowers of the evergreen strawberry tree or arbutus shrub (*Arbutus unedo*) found in southern Europe, northwest parts of North America, and Canada. Dark in color, it has a strong, bitter/sweet complex flavor.

Sweet salt from Cervia

A sea salt extracted through natural evaporation that creates a rich depth of flavor. Hailing from Cervia, in the region of Emilia-Romagna, this highly prized salt is described as being "sweet," because it lacks bitter minerals and contains no additives. The purity of its sodium chloride makes it naturally more "sweet" than other sea salts.

To truss

To tie a bird, such as chicken, with kitchen twine so the wings and legs stay close to the body. This ensures the bird is compact and helps it cook evenly. Place the bird breast-side-up with the legs facing you. Put the center of the twine directly beneath the tailbone of the bird. Lift the twine around the legs, make a cross, and pull the two ends tort so the legs come together. Pull the ends of the twine forward, around the front of the bird, and over the wings. Turn the bird breast-side-down, pull the twine tort and tie a knot at the neck.

Vernaccia wine

An Italian dry white wine made from the Vernaccia grape, which is produced in and around the town of San Gimignanao in Tuscany. It holds Denominazione di Origine Controllata e Garantita (DOCG) status and has a crisp, fresh, and fruity flavor with citrus notes. It works well with pork and poultry.

Venison

Venison tends to refer to deer meat, which is championed for its rich and gamey flavor. In the UK, most farmed deer meat comes from red deer. Venison is widely available across Europe but less common in the United States, where it tends to be imported from New Zealand. Cuts of venison are suitable for roasts, steaks, and ground (minced) meat.

Wild boar

Also known as wild hogs, wild pigs, or feral swine.

Woodcock or snipe

The woodcock is a small migratory wading bird that is recognizable by its long beak. A rare bird, if it can be found the woodcock is highly desirable as game, but hunting it is controlled, subject to strict quotas, and selling it on the open market is forbidden.

Phaidon Press Limited
Regent's Wharf
All Saints Street
London N1 9PA

Phaidon Press Inc.
65 Bleecker Street
New York, NY 10012

phaidon.com

First published 2017
© 2017 Phaidon Press Limited

ISBN: 978 0 7148 7497 5

Recipes from an Italian Butcher originates
from *Il cucchiaio d'argento*, first published
in 1950, tenth edition (revised, expanded
and updated in 2016), *Il cucchiaio
d'argento arrosti irresistibili*, first published
in 2014, *Il cucchiaio d'argento piccoli
arrosti*, first published in 2016, *Il cucchiaio
d'argento carni da i secondi piatti*, first
published in 2004, and *Il cucchiaio
d'argento scuola di cucina arrosti, brasati
e polpettoni*, first published in 2013.
© Editoriale Domus S.p.A

A CIP catalogue record for this book is
available from the British Library and the
Library of Congress.

Commissioning Editor: Emilia Terragni
Project Editor: Sophie Hodgkin
Production Controller: Matthew Harvey

Introduction by Gregor Shepherd
Photography by Simon Bajada
Design by Hyperkit

The publisher would also like to thank
Theresa Bebbington, Carmen Figini,
Oskar Montano, Kathy Steer, and Hilary
Bird for their contributions to the book.

Printed in China

Recipe Notes

Butter should always be salted.

All herbs are fresh, unless otherwise specified.

Individual vegetables and fruits, such as onions and apples, are
assumed to be medium, unless otherwise specified.

Eggs are assumed to be large (UK medium), unless otherwise
specified.

Cooking times are for guidance only, as individual ovens vary.
If using a fan (convection) oven, follow the manufacturer's
instructions concerning oven temperatures.

Exercise a high level of caution when following recipes involving
any potentially hazardous activity, including the use of high
temperatures, open flames and when deep-frying. In particular,
when deep-frying, add food carefully to avoid splashing, wear
long sleeves and never leave the pan unattended.

When using an earthenware pot on the stove (hob) or in the oven,
avoid quick changes of temperature because they may cause
the clay to crack. Always use a heat diffuser when cooking with
earthenware pots on an electric or ceramic stove.

Some recipes include raw or very lightly cooked eggs, meat or fish,
and fermented products. These should be avoided by the elderly,
infants, pregnant women, convalescents, and anyone with an
impaired immune system.

Exercise caution when making fermented products, ensuring
all equipment is spotlessly clean, and seek expert advice if in
any doubt.

All herbs, shoots, flowers and leaves (greens) should be picked
fresh from a clean source. Exercise caution when foraging for
ingredients; any foraged ingredients should only be eaten if
an expert has deemed them safe to eat.

When no quantity is specified, for example of oils, salts and herbs
used for finishing dishes, quantities are discretionary and flexible.

Both metric and imperial measures are used in this book. Follow
one set of measurements throughout, not a mixture, as they are
not interchangeable.

All spoon and cup measurements are level, unless otherwise stated.
1 teaspoon = 5 ml; 1 tablespoon = 15 ml.

Australian standard tablespoons are 20 ml, so Australian readers
are advised to use 3 teaspoons in place of 1 tablespoon when
measuring small quantities.